SUSTAINABLE
COMMUNITY-OWNED
ENTERPRISES

JOHN MAKILYA

 ARCHWAY
PUBLISHING

Archway Publishing books may be ordered through booksellers or by contacting:

Archway Publishing
1663 Liberty Drive
Bloomington, IN 47403
www.archwaypublishing.com
1 (888) 242-5904

Interior Image Credit: John Makilya

ISBN: 978-1-4808-9474-7 (sc)
ISBN: 978-1-4808-9473-0 (e)

Library of Congress Control Number: 2020915999

Print information available on the last page.

Archway Publishing rev. date: 11/13/2020

DEDICATION

I dedicate this book to my wife, Petronilla (Nilla), my daughters Jacqueline, Maureen, and Eve, and my son, John Paul (JP), for their love, encouragement, support, patience, and care during difficult times when we lived in Kenya and in the US.

Many times, I left my family behind and crisscrossed Kenya as I supervised various projects and programs in the country from the beef-producing lowlands around Voi and the fertile horticulture-growing Taita Hills to the shores of Lake Turkana; from the hot and humid Lake Victoria basin to the cooler coffee-growing highlands in central and eastern Kenya; from the dairy, pyrethrum (a plant whose flowers make insecticides), and coffee-growing areas in Kisii to the nomadic communities in the Rift Valley; from the Shimoni, Mkwiro, and Kibuyuni fishing communities in south coastal Kenya to the communities in wildlife areas in the Laikipia, Samburu, and Baringo Districts; and from the group ranches bordering the Amboseli National Park to the group ranches in Maasai Mara not to mention time spent in other countries including mainland Tanzania, the island of Zanzibar, and countries including Rwanda, Burundi, Germany (Frankfurt), Sweden (Copenhagen), and the United States (Connecticut and Massachusetts).

Thank you for bearing with me as I spent all that time away from you attending to the various responsibilities of my job. Indeed, the time I spent in all these places without you can never be adequately compensated. My consolation, however, is the satisfaction I get when I consider the benefits that accrued to the beneficiary communities as a result of my work.

Moreover, you continued to strengthen and provide me encouragement even as I was writing this book and going through the ups and downs of life in the US. May almighty God pour his blessings on all of you as you continue pursuing your goals.

FOREWORD

Community-owned enterprises use business concepts to improve the life of a community. Sustainable community-owned enterprises do so in a way that does not compromise the ability of the enterprises to meet the needs of future generations.

The book starts with an overview of the diminishing employment benefits in the corporate world sparked by use of technology, which has disrupted various industries. What we are witnessing today with Uber and Lyft as alternatives to taxis is a good example. Through use of technology, Airbnb has disrupted the hotel industry by providing reasonably priced accommodations to guests.

Other sectors that technological innovation will disrupt include doctors' office visits, financial and legal services, health care diagnostics, education, data protection, customer service, insurance, the automotive industry, the security industry, and paper pushers such as real estate or roadside assistance services.

In advanced counties, the tendency is for people to be self-employed if they cannot be absorbed in the new organizations. In developing countries, the better option is to form and strengthen existing community-owned enterprises so they can provide sustainable benefits to their members.

This book offers the attributes of a sustainable community-owned enterprise as follows.

- Ownership must be by members of a community.
- No member should own more than 5 percent of the equity of the community activity.
- Each member should have equal voting rights.

- Management, accounting, and financial control systems must be designed and implemented by competent personnel who are trained to use the systems.
- A system of distribution of profits and benefits must be in place and understood by members.
- Bylaws should spell out the qualifications necessary for membership and election to management committees, the functions of management committee (subcommittees where necessary), and management committee relations with operational management.
- Bylaws must also specify duties and responsibilities of members.
- Bylaws should provide for regular management committee meetings to review among other items monthly accounts and the business of the community. The manager of the community activity must sit at all committee meetings and act as secretary to the committee.

Examples of sustainable community-owned enterprises can be found in a variety of economic sectors including savings and credit cooperatives, ranching and the beef industry in coastal Kenya, sustainable community-owned and -operated water projects, horticultural production and marketing, fishing enterprises, milk processing, coffee-processing and -marketing enterprises, and wildlife conservation using the resources of community-owned tourist facilities.

This book demonstrates methods of evaluating the effectiveness of infrastructural interventions in communities' projects through studies including the socioeconomic assessments of the World Bank–funded El Niño Emergency Project, the Special Assistance for Project Implementation (SAPI) funded by Japan International Cooperation Assistance (JICA), and the Horticultural Producing Facilities Project under the Horticultural Crops Development Authority (HCDA).

There are examples of unsuccessful community enterprises in the sugar industry, which had been successful under the plantation model but unsuccessful under smallholder production in Kenya. Sugar production and marketing modeled on smallholder coffee production and marketing in the Central and Eastern provinces has been unsuccessful as well. The sugar industry is the only sector, over several decades, where the community-owned enterprise model has not been successful.

CONTENTS

CHAPTER 1

SUSTAINABLE COMMUNITY-
OWNED ENTERPRISES

What does *sustainable* mean? According to James D. Wolfensohn, president of the World Bank Group,

> Corporate sustainability today includes recognition of the leadership role that the private sector must take in ensuring social progress, improved equity, higher living standards, and stewardship for the environment. Corporate responsibility is not philanthropy—it is good business.[1]

When we manage any resource base to at least maintain if not increase our quality of life and that of future generations, we are practicing sustainability. Our generation's management of the resource base is sustainable if it constitutes the first part of feasible sustainable development.

[1] Corporate sustainability today includes recognition of the leadership role that the private sector must take in ensuring social progress, improved equity, higher living standards, and stewardship for the environment. Corporate responsibility is not philanthropy—it is good business.

The World Commission on Environment and Development's 1987 publication "Our Common Future" states,

> Sustainable development is development that meets the needs of the present without compromising the ability of future generations to meet their own needs. It contains within it two key concepts:
>
> - The concept of "needs," in particular, the essential needs of the world's poor, to which overriding priority should be given; and
> - The idea of limitations imposed by the state of technology and social organization on the environment's ability to meet present and future needs.

> A community is a group of living things sharing the same environment with usually shared interests. In human communities, people have some of the same beliefs and needs, and this affects the identity of the group and the people in it.[2]

> Community-based enterprises use business to improve the life of a community. A business activity is undertaken as a means of achieving community benefit.[3]

GROUP/COMMUNITY-OWNED ORGANIZATIONS AND ENTERPRISES

Group activities started in Kenya between 1400 and 1500, when Kenyan tribes settled in Kenya. Group activities included the following.

---

[2] Wikipedia.

[3] http://www.communitypartnering.info/what45.html.

Firewood Harvesting and Water Collection

Women in certain villages or women married into a particular clan would organize to harvest firewood. The advantage of such group harvesting was the belief that wildlife would rarely attack a group of women. During periods of intertribal war, women would harvest firewood in groups under the protection of warriors from their community. Once the women were escorted back to their homes with the firewood, the warriors would resume their intertribal war.

Group firewood harvesting activities took place prior to a *ntheo* (marriage) party; the families of those being married were expected to host and cook for major receptions. Groups of women would also harvest firewood prior to a major clan elders' meeting or when they expected visits of members of their clan coming from a distant place.

Communities in Kenya settled in different phases. Usually, an advance party went ahead in search of good agricultural or pasture land and sent back word for the others to follow. Their arrival was celebrated with a party for which the women would gather firewood for cooking.

Groups of women, usually younger women who were breastfeeding, fetched water. Usually, they collected water from nearby sources so they would not be gone from their infants for long. Women whose children were older could travel farther to collect firewood. Those who fetched water at times would have their infants strapped to their breasts and gourds of water strapped to their backs.

Weeding and Harvesting Groups

Among communities that practiced agriculture and raising livestock, women were responsible for agricultural production. The women would weed and harvest the gardens of each woman in turn.

They were the providers of agricultural foodstuffs for their families; those who did not participate in such work would be sanctioned and even divorced by their husbands. Divorce in Kenyan communities in those days was a very serious matter as marriage was regarded as a binding relationship between the family of the bride and that of the groom. A divorced woman was regarded also as a disgrace to her family as she was associated with laziness and noncompliance with accepted community behavior. Moreover, a divorced woman had no land rights at her parents' home and therefore no livelihood.

The voluntary community groups formed on clan and village levels functioned very well and were regulated by the community's social norms or censorship.

Changes were, however, introduced by the colonial government under the Chief's Authority Act of 1934. Under this act, chiefs were authorized to coerce people and groups to take part in certain communal activities. People would be coerced to provide labor to construct roads, schools, and dams with severe penalties for noncompliance.

The next phase of group formations and activities was promoted by the requirement to form marketing cooperatives to market coffee for small-scale producers in the 1950s. However, it was not until Kenyan independence that there was a marked growth of marketing cooperatives and community organizations.

After Kenya achieved independence in 1963, the growth of community organizations was promoted by the founder of the Kenyan nation, Mzee Jomo Kenyatta, through what he introduced as Harambee, which means "all pull together" in Swahili; it is the motto of Kenya and appears on its coat of arms. It is a Kenyan tradition of community self-help events such as fundraising and development activities. Harambee events range from informal affairs lasting a few hours, for which invitations are spread by word of mouth, to formal, multiday events advertised in newspapers. These events have long been important in parts of East Africa as ways of building and maintaining communities.

Following Kenya's independence, the first prime minister and later first president of Kenya Jomo Kenyatta adopted Harambee as a concept of pulling the country together to build a new nation. He encouraged communities to work together to raise funds for all sorts of local projects, and he pledged that the government would provide their startup costs. Under this system, wealthy individuals wishing to get into politics could donate large amounts of money to local harambee drives thereby gaining legitimacy; however, such practices were never institutionalized during Kenyatta's presidency.

Despite these criticisms of Harambee, there has been a great growth in group activity in Kenya. With growth, however, came challenges as noted under the Harambee slogan, which saw a lot of activities spring up and abuses attendant to their immense growth.

However, on a good note, the '60s and '70s saw the growth of more marketing cooperatives for coffee, pyrethrum, milk, tea, horticulture, fishing, and other products. These started and continue to operate like community-owned enterprises. Some have granted great benefits to their members while others have failed. Other group organizations outside cooperatives include water users' associations, group ranches, wildlife-related enterprises, and so on.

In conclusion, sustainable community-based enterprises are business activities undertaken as a means of achieving a community benefit now and in the future.

This book looks at community-based businesses with which the author has had on-the-ground experiences with. The author believes that for the community-based enterprises to be sustainable, they must have the following attributes.

- Ownership must be by members of a community.
- No member should own more than 5 percent of the equity of the community activity.
- Each member should have equal voting rights.
- Management, accounting, and financial control systems must be designed and implemented by competent personnel trained in the systems.
- A system for distributing profits and benefits must be in place and understood by members.
- Bylaws should spell out qualifications for membership and election to management positions, the functions of the management committee and any subcommittees, and management committee relations with operational management.
- Bylaws should specify the duties and responsibilities of members.
- Bylaws should provide for regular management committee meetings to review among other items accounts and the business of the community. The manager of the community activity must sit at all committee meetings and act as secretary to the committee.

A community-owned enterprise might have all these attributes, but the moment its management committee fails to equitably distribute benefits to the members, the enterprise can start disintegrating. At one annual meeting of such an enterprise, auditors revealed that the committee had misappropriated the benefits due for distribution to members, but surprisingly, some of the membership shouted, "Remove the committee and replace them with other members! Don't report the matter to the police. The resources of this enterprise belong to us, not the police!" That enterprise collapsed the following year.

CHAPTER 2

THE CHANGING GLOBAL LABOR MARKET

Technology has caused total disruption in the employment sectors of developed and developing countries alike. This disruption has prompted people to seek sustainable self-employment as traditional jobs seem to be dwindling. Even where the jobs are not disappearing, many companies have used technology to disrupt existing businesses to the extent of driving some out of business. Employment now comes with few if any benefits.

Technology in developed countries has been a major cause of the reduction of traditional jobs. In stores like Stop & Shop and Walmart, you find self-checkout counters have increased and several automated produce robots have been introduced. Clothing stores, even during holiday seasons, have fewer checkout stations, and even when long lines form, these quickly die out after a few minutes. Many people are shopping online for clothing and even groceries.

Employers are replacing older employees with younger employees whose salaries are much less. Every month, the government reports reductions in the level of unemployment, but the situation on the ground is that many hourly employees, especially in stores, work fewer than forty hours a week, so they have to work two or three jobs to pay their bills.

Many employers have moved away from defined-benefit plans (pensions) whereby the employer is responsible for providing a specific amount of money to the employee upon retirement. The pension plans have been replaced with defined-contribution retirement plans. The employee and employer may make contributions to the plan up to the dollar limits set by the Internal Revenue Service. Some employers match the employees' contribution while others do not. Other benefits that have been reduced include health coverage, leaving the employee to shoulder higher deductible amounts to get health care.

Airbnbs, or air mattress bed-and-breakfasts according to Investopedia, is an online marketplace that connects people who want to rent out their homes to guests who will visit their areas. Airbnb is estimated to be worth about $38 billion according to what a source close to the company told Vox in March 2019 and what *Forbes* estimated in March 2018. Airbnb is giving the hotel industry a run for its money.

Uber is posing a challenge to taxis. Unlike the taxi business, where the owners buy the taxis, Uber does not invest in vehicles; it is a car-for-hire service that relies on smartphone technology to dispatch drivers, who use their own cars. In June 2019, Uber was a $3.166 billion revenue company.

A business similar to Uber is Lyft. Founded in June 2012 and based in San Francisco, it operating in 644 cities in the United States and Puerto Rico and nine cities in Canada. It develops, markets, and operates the Lyft mobile app offering car rides, scooters, a bicycle-sharing system, and a food delivery service. Like Uber, it does not own any of the vehicles. Lyft was worth $15.1 billion (as of December 2018), making it a quarter of the value of its competitor, Uber.

Amazon is an American multinational technology company based in Seattle that focuses on e-commerce, cloud computing, digital streaming, and artificial intelligence (AI). It is considered one of the big-four tech companies along with Google, Apple, and Facebook. It is known for its disruption of well-established industries through technological innovation and mass scale. It is the world's largest online marketplace, AI provider, and cloud-computing platform as measured by revenue and market capitalization. It is the largest internet company by revenue in the world. It is the second-largest private employer in the United States and one of the world's most valuable companies.

Amazon employees who work more than twenty hours per week receive benefits, including life and disability insurance, dental and vision insurance with premiums paid in full by Amazon and funding toward medical insurance. However, part-time employees may have problems averaging twenty hours a week as their schedules fluctuate between peak and low seasons. Peak periods during the year are usually around holidays such as Valentine's Day, Easter, Halloween, Thanksgiving, and Christmas; other periods are low seasons. Because of fluctuations in hours worked, employees may find it difficult to average twenty hours per week and thus are excluded from the above benefits.

HUMAN AUGMENTATION (TECHNOLOGY)

According to *Instant* magazine, technology has always augmented human capabilities going back to the time of the Industrial Revolution, but so far, this has been relatively passive—only assisting humans in performing tasks.

However, the role of technology has changed from passive to active; it works alongside us and directly on our behalf. New developments currently include AI, augmented reality (AR), virtual reality (VR), sensors, and blockchain technology. These breakthroughs are in turn generating new products and services such as AVs, drones, and robots.

Human-augmentation technologies include self-driving cars and the automation of jobs such as retail purchases. It is anticipated that augmentation will blur the line between humans and machines by challenging entrenched perceptions we have of ourselves.

Technology continues to disrupt almost every business sector with constant advancements and amazing new use cases. No industry is immune to the impact of technology; however, some are more prone to major change than others. Let us look at the ten areas below where disruption is just a matter of time.

1. Doctor's Office Visits

Health care providers are looking for ways to create more opportunities for self-care and preventive care because of changing demographics in the population, reimbursement changes, and uncertainty about the customers' ability to pay and their stability. The traditional office visit is ripe for disruption.

2. Financial and Legal Services

The increasingly intelligent chatbots for customer service, machine learning for fraud detection and contract analysis, blockchain for moving money through the system, and cognitive search and analytics for providing key stakeholders with relevant information and insights are all clear indications of the imminent disruption in the traditional provision of financial and legal services.

3. Healthcare Diagnostics

Artificial intelligence (AI), Internet of Things, and mobile devices are combining to drive improvements in the collection and analysis of health care data. They are moving diagnostics from hospitals to our homes, leveraging AI to screen cancer with a mobile app, and discovering health anomalies from data collected by wearable devices. This disruption will only hasten as technological improvements revolutionize preventive care.

4. Education

Education will move toward personalization as the current mass approach to education is not serving our kids. We are witnessing a move to finding out the unique interests of children and letting them explore that curiosity in other subjects.

5. Data Protection

For years, we have seen headlines with data protection and privacy without any significant pushback from cybersecurity vendors. Solutions were based on endpoints or networks. There is a move to see the adoption of data-centric solutions protecting data in all forms, across all devices, including the cloud. It is predicted that IT will have full visibility, security, and control of data, just as if the data were on a central file server.

6. Customer Service

Today, the customer service industry is ripe for disruption as it does not require a behavior change. Under current customer service, people interact visually and contextually, but flexibly leveraging a combination of traditional voice and digital communications will change the market place. With the right technology, it can respond to the smartphone and on-demand behavior change that has already taken place over the past five years.

7. Insurance

Some insurance companies have entered the FinTech space as inspiration for digitization. With FinTech partnerships, insurers can operate at lower costs, alleviate reliance on legacy systems, and improve the customer experience with user-centric mobile products. The opportunity to introduce customer value with mobile solutions now exists.

8. Automotive Industry

Autonomous vehicles now in the market are clear signs that the automotive industry is ripe for disruption. We have started to see traditional manufacturing companies morph into tech organizations. Like every other sector, the auto industry is learning to use the latest innovations to streamline processes.

9. Security

The coming years will be years of security analytics and machine learning. Next year the innovators in this field will begin to dominate and grow. Expect acquisitions as those who don't have their footing attempt to gain relevancy in the space. This is the time to invest in machine learning security startups, especially those that solve expensive, time-consuming security questions in moments.

10. "Paper Pushers"

Keep an eye on all industries with heavy paper pushing or phone call–based processes, such as real estate or roadside assistance. There are tangible signs that very soon there will be mainstream adoption and transformation in either Brokerage Engine and Mach1 or both of those markets.[4]

Threatened by disruptions, business owners have resorted to measures including amalgamations to avoid being phased out of business. There is also an increased need for more and more people to start their own businesses to avoid losing incomes if their employers go out of business.

WHAT IS THE CASE IN DEVELOPING COUNTRIES?

Traditional jobs in developing countries are also on the decline. In Kenya, the whole textile industry has crashed. In the last twenty or so years, Kenya has witnessed the closure of listed companies including Rivatex, KICOMI, Thika Cloth Mills, Juja Sisal, Kenya Meat Corporation, Kenya Reinsurance, Postal Corporation of Kenya, and Kenya National Assurance. All sugar processing companies are also on the verge of collapse. The reasons include corruption

---

[4] Points 1 to 10 came from *Forbes*.

driving the cost of input high, spiraling costs of production, inefficient production methods, competition from overseas suppliers, or a combination of these factors.

WHERE DOES THE KENYAN ECONOMY STAND AS AN EMPLOYMENT PROVIDER?

In 2019, Kenya had an estimated population of 52.6 million compared to a population of 8.1 million in 1960. According to UN projections, Kenya's population will grow by around 1 million per year, 3,000 people every day, for the next forty years and will reach about 85 million by 2050.

As of 2019, Kenya had an estimated GDP of $99.246 billion and per capita GDP of $2,010 making it the sixty-second largest economy in the world. Its economy enjoys the leading position in eastern and central Africa, but almost 17 percent of its population lives below the poverty line; the solution to poverty in Kenya still needs long-term efforts.

Official data shows that the proportion of Kenyans living in poverty has fallen by 10.5 percent to 36.1 percent. The Kenya National Bureau of Statistics (KNBS) attributes the drop to economic expansion and devolution of resources to local authorities (June 28, 2018).

> Kenya has been ranked eighth globally and sixth in Africa among countries with the largest number of people living in extreme poverty, according to the World Poverty Clock report. The report says that 29 per cent (14.7 million) of the 49,684,304 people are very poor as they consume less than $1.90 (Sh197) per day or Sh5,910 monthly. With a poverty escape rate of 0.5 people per minute, the drive to achieve the United Nation's Sustainable Development Goals (SDGs) is at risk. UN's SDGs aim at reducing the number of people living in extreme poverty by 2030. According to the report, Turkana has the largest number of people living below the poverty line with 87.4 per cent (756,306) and a poverty escape rate of -1.1 people/hour.[5]

---

[5] https://www.businessdailyafrica.com/economy/Kenya-8th-on-extreme-poverty-list/3946234-4635310-79pa9rz/index.html.

The economy of Kenya is a market-based economy with a liberalized external trade system and a few state enterprises. Major industries include agriculture, forestry, fishing, mining, manufacturing, energy, tourism and financial services. As of 2019, Kenya had an estimated GDP of $99.246 billion and per capita GDP of $2,010 making it the 62nd largest economy in the world.[6]

Let us look at Kenya's economic history before we dive into sustainable community-owned enterprises.

Economic History

The Kenyan coastal strip was integrated into the world economy by ancient world trade routes that spanned Africa, Asia and Europe between 70 AD and 1500 AD.[1] Foreign merchants brought their merchandise to Kenyan coast and left with African goods.[2] In 1499 AD, Vasco da Gama returned from discovering the sea route to India through South Africa.[3] This new route allowed European nations to dominate the trade economy of the East African coast, with the Portuguese entrenching themselves in the 16th and 17th centuries.[4] In the 18th century the Portuguese were replaced in this East African economic corridor by Omani Arabs.[5] Eventually, the British replaced the Omani Arabs. In 1895 they dominated the coastal strip, and by 1920 they had followed the interior trade routes all the way to the Buganda Kingdom [6]. To make this ancient economic trade route more profitable, the British used Indian laborers to build a railway from Mombasa at the coast to Kampala, the capital of Buganda kingdom, following the old trade route.[7, 8] Major towns were founded along the railway line, backed by European settler farming communities. The Indian laborers who did not return to India after railway

---

6 https://www.quora.com/Why-does-Kenyas-capital-Nairobi-look-so-futuristic-with-skyscrapers-etc-when-the- country-is-so-poor v.

construction ended were the first to establish shops (dukawallahs) in these towns.[9] During the colonial period, the European settler farming community and the Indian dukawallahs established the foundations of the modern formal Kenyan economy.[10] Prominent examples of Asian-Kenyan business owners whose businesses started as dukawallahs include Manu Chandaria and Madatally Manji.[11] While Europeans and Indians enjoyed strong economic growth between 1920 and 1963, Africans were deprived of their land, dehumanized and forced to work for minimal pay under extremely poor working conditions through a well-established system of racial segregation.[12]

Kenya regained its independence in 1963. Under President Jomo Kenyatta, the Kenyan government promoted africanization of the Kenyan economy,[22] generating rapid economic growth through public investment, encouragement of smallholder agricultural production, and incentives for private, often foreign, industrial investment. An influential sessional paper authored by Tom Mboya and Mwai Kibaki in 1965 stressed the need for Kenya to avoid both the capitalistic economy of the West and the communism of the East.[23] The paper argued that Kenya should instead concentrate on African socialism, while avoiding linking Kenya's economic fortunes to any country or group of countries.[23] From 1963 to 1973 gross domestic product (GDP) grew at an annual average rate of 6.6%, and during the 1970s it grew at an average rate of 7.2%. Agricultural production grew by 4.7% annually during the same period, stimulated by redistributing estates, distributing new crop strains, and opening new areas to cultivation. However, the rate of GDP growth declined to 4.2% per year in the 1980s, and 2.2% a year in the 1990s.[24]

Kenya's policy of import substitution, which started in 1946 with European and Asian enterprises, did not achieve the desired result of transforming Kenya's industrial base, and in the late 1970s rising oil prices began to make Kenya's manufacturing sector noncompetitive.[25] In response, the government began a massive intervention in the private sector. Lack of export incentives, tight import controls, and foreign exchange controls made the domestic environment for investment even less attractive. From 1991 to 1993, Kenya had its worst economic performance since independence. Growth in GDP stagnated, and agricultural production shrank at an annual rate of 3.9%. Inflation reached a record of 100% in August 1993, and the government's budget deficit was over 10% of GDP.[26] As a result of these issues, bilateral and multilateral donors suspended their aid programs in Kenya in 1991.[27]

In the 1980s and 1990s, at the height of the Daniel arap Moi administration, the introduction of structural adjustment programs (SAPs) sponsored by the IMF and World Bank contributed to the decline and two-decade stagnation of Kenya's economy.[28] Some of the conditions of the SAPs, such as structural adjustment loans and strict conditions regarding government policy, resulted in a decrease in government spending on economic and social services, a decrease in educational enrollment, and an increase in unemployment (especially in the agricultural industry). The loans were also used to pay off other debts.[29] As a result, the formal economy gave way to the growth of the informal economy, living standards began to decline, and Kenya opened up to the global economy.[30]

In 1993, the Government of Kenya began a major program of economic reform and liberalization. A new minister of finance and a new governor of the central bank undertook a series of economic measures with the assistance of the World Bank and the International Monetary Fund (IMF). As part of this program, the government eliminated price controls and import licensing, removed foreign exchange controls, privatized a number of publicly owned companies, reduced the number of civil servants, and introduced conservative fiscal and monetary policies.[31] From

1994 to 1996, Kenya's real GDP growth rate averaged just over 4% a year.[32]

Kenya's Economic Performance Since Independence

In 1997, however, the economy entered a period of slowing or stagnant growth, due in part to adverse weather conditions and reduced economic activity before the general elections in December 1997. In July 1997, the Government of Kenya refused to meet earlier commitments to the IMF on governance reforms.[33] As a result, the IMF suspended lending for three years, and the World Bank also put a $90 million structural adjustment credit on hold.[34]

The Government of Kenya subsequently took positive steps on reform, including the establishment of the Kenya Anti-Corruption Authority in 1997, and measures to improve the transparency of government procurement and reduce the government payroll. In July 2000, the IMF signed a $150 million Poverty Reduction and Growth Facility, and the World Bank followed shortly after with a $157 million Economic and Public Sector Reform credit. However, both were suspended.[34]

Economic growth improved between 2003 and 2008, under the Mwai Kibaki administration.[35] When Kibaki took power in 2003, he immediately established the National Debt Management Department at the treasury, reformed the Kenya Revenue Authority (KRA) to increase government revenue, reformed financial laws on banking, wrote off the debts of strategic public enterprises and ensured that 30% of government tax revenue was invested in economic development projects. With these National Rainbow Coalition (NARC) government-driven reforms, the KRA collected more tax revenue in 2004 than was anticipated. The government then initiated investments in infrastructure. By 2005, the Kenyan public debt had reduced from highs of 80% of GDP in 2002 to 27% of GDP in 2005. The financial sector greatly improved, and Equity

Bank Kenya Limited became one of the largest banks in East Africa. Economic growth improved from 2% in 2003 to 7% in 2007.[36] In 2008, the growth slumped to 1%[37] due to post-election violence before returning to an average of 5% between 2009 and 2013.[38][39]

Between 2013 and 2018 under the Jubilee Party government led by Uhuru Kenyatta, GDP growth averaged above 5%.[40][41] Growth in small businesses is credited with some of the improvement.[42] Real GDP growth (annualized) was 5.7% in Q1 of 2018, 6.0% in Q2 2018 and 6.2% in Q3 2018.[43] Despite this robust growth, concerns remain on Kenya's debt sustainability, current account deficit, fiscal consolidation and revenue growth.[44, 45]

The table below shows the GDP of Kenya estimated by the International Monetary Fund, with exchange rates for Kenyan shillings.

Year	Nominal GDP	(USD)US Dollar Exchange
1980	7.265 Billion	7.42 Shillings
1985	6.135 Billion	16.43 Shillings
1990	8.591 Billion	22.86 Shillings
1995	9.046 Billion	50.42 Shillings
2000	12.71 Billion	78.58 Shillings
2005	18.74 Billion	75.55 Shillings
2010	40 Billion	78.90 Shillings
2015	63.77 Billion	96.85 Shillings
2018	85.98 Billion	100.77 Shillings
2020--		

Economic Planning: Kenya Vision 2030

Vision 2030 is Kenya's current blueprint for the future of economic growth. Its goal is to create a prosperous, and globally competitive nation with a high quality of life by the year 2030. To do this, it aims to transform Kenyan industry while creating a clean and secure environment. The vision is separated into three pillars: economic, social, and political.[46, 47]

The Economic Pillar

The economic pillar seeks to consistently achieve economic growth averaging more than 10% for 23 years beginning in the year 2007. The economic areas targeted are tourism, agriculture, wholesale/retail trade, manufacturing, IT-enabled services, and financial services.[48]

The Social Pillar

The social pillar has the objective of improving the quality of life for all Kenyans. It aims to do this by targeting human and social welfare programs, specifically education and training, health, environment, housing and urbanization, children and social development, and youth and sports.[49] In 2018 President Uhuru Kenyatta established the Big Four Agenda, focusing on universal health care, manufacturing, affordable housing and food security, to drive this pillar.

The Political Pillar

The political pillar envisions a democratic system that is issue-based, people-centered, results-oriented and is accountable to the public. It targets five main areas: the rule of law under the Constitution of Kenya; electoral and political processes; democracy and public service delivery; transparency and accountability; and security, peacebuilding and conflict management.[50]

Currency, Exchange Rate, and Inflation

The exchange rate of the Kenya shilling, KSh, between 2003 and 2010 averaged about KSh74-78 to US$1.[51] The average inflation between 2005 and July 2015 was 8.5%.[52] In July 2015, Kenya's inflation rate was estimated to be 6.62%.[53]

Kenya's currency is printed by mandate of the Central Bank of Kenya.[54] The bank began printing banknotes in 1996. Several versions of Kenya's banknotes and coinage have been launched into circulation since then. The most recent redesign of Kenya's currency was in 2019.[54]

Government Finances—Revenue and Spending

In 2006, Kenya's government revenues totaled US$4.448 billion and its estimated expenditures totaled US$5.377B. Government budget balance as a percentage of gross domestic product had improved to −2.1% in 2006 from −5.5% in 2004.[55]

In 2012, Kenya set a budget of US$14.59B with a government revenue of approximately US$12B.[56]

The 2018 budget policy report set a budget of US$30B. Government revenue averaged US$25B. The deficit of US$5B was borrowed.[57]

Government Debt

From 1982, Kenya key public debt indicators rose above the critical level measured as a percentage of GDP and as a percentage of government revenue.[58]

In 2002, the last year of Daniel arap Moi's administration, Kenya's public debt stood at almost 80% of GDP. In the last 10 years of the Moi regime, the government was spending 94% of all its revenue on salaries and debt servicing to IMF, World Bank and other western countries.[59] In 2003, Mwai Kibaki's administration instituted a public debt management department within the treasury department to bring Kenya's debt down to sustainable levels.[60]

In 2006, Kenya had a current account deficit of US$1.5B. This figure was a significant increase over 2005, when the current account had a deficit of US$495 million. In 2006, the current account balance as a percentage of gross domestic product was −4.2.[55]

In 2006 Kenya's external debt totaled US$6.7B. With a GDP of US$25.83B in 2006, the public debt level stood at 27% of GDP.[55]

In 2011 debt management report the national treasury noted that the debt was rising, growing to 40% of GDP in 2009 and to 54% of GDP by 2012.[62]

In 2019, Kenya's debt had risen to an absolute amount of US$50B against a GDP of US$98B. The public debt level is thus 51% of GDP as of 2019.[62] Kenya's largest bilateral lender since 2011 has been China, and the largest multilateral lender since 1963 has been the World Bank.[63]

Kenya Economic Stimulus Program

The Kenya Economic Stimulus Program (ESP) was introduced in the 2010/2011 budget plan.[64] The initiative aimed to stimulate economic activity in Kenya through investment in long term solutions to the challenges of food security, rural unemployment and underdevelopment. Its stated objective was to promote regional development for equity and social stability, improving infrastructure, enhancing the quality of education, availing affordable health-care for all Kenyans, investing in the conservation of the environment, building Kenya's Information and communications technology (ICT) capacity and expanding access to ICT for the general populace of Kenya.[65] The Ministry of Finance aimed to use this program to achieve regional development for equity and social stability.

Integrated Financial Management Information System

Originally introduced in 2003, the Integrated Financial Management Information System (IFMIS)[66] was reengineered by the Ministry of Finance to curb fraud and other malpractices. In doing this, the Ministry aimed to put Kenya's financial and economic information in a format that was accessible from an online platform, to improve management of public expenditures by the Ministry of Finance.

IFMIS enables fully integrated planning for the budgeting process since it links planning policy objectives and budget allocation.[67] It also seeks to support the e-Government shared services strategy by taking government financial services online and making status reports readily available. The system offers improvements in planning and budgeting, monitoring, evaluation and accountability and budget execution.

Funds for the Inclusion of Informal Sector

The Fund for the Inclusion of Informal Sector (FIIS)[68] is a fund that allows micro and small entrepreneurs (MSE) to access credit facilities, expand their businesses and increase their savings. It also aims to help informal enterprises transition to formal sector enterprises, through access to formal providers of financial services. FIIS is a revolving fund through which the government enters into credit facility agreements with select banks for lending to micro-and-small-enterprises through branches, authorized banking agents and other channels, particularly mobile banking. An estimated 8.3 million Kenyans work in the informal sector.

Investor Compensation Fund

The Investor Compensation Fund is intended to compensate investors who suffer losses resulting from failure of a licensed stockbroker or dealer to meet his/her contractual obligations, up to a maximum of Sh.50, 000 per investor.

Foreign Economic Relations

Kenyan exports in 2006

Since independence, Kenya has received both substantial foreign investment and significant amounts of development aid. Total aid was $943 million in 2006, which was 4% of gross national income.[69] These investments come from Russia, China, the developed Western countries and Japan. Kenya hosts a large number of foreign multinational companies, as well as international organizations such as United Nations Environment Program (UNEP) and many other non-governmental organizations [70]. China's involvement has been increasing, while that of Western countries such as the United Kingdom has fallen significantly. Investments from multilateral agencies, particularly the World Bank and the European Development Fund, have increased. The most active investors currently are the Chinese.

Kenya is active within regional trade blocs such as the Common Market for Eastern and Southern Africa (COMESA) and the East African Community (EAC), a partnership of Kenya, Uganda, and Tanzania. The aim of the EAC is to create a common market of the three states modelled on the European Union.[55] Among the early steps toward integration is the customs union which has eliminated duties on goods and non-tariff trade barriers among the members.

Exports

Kenya's chief exports are horticultural products and tea. In 2005, the combined value of these commodities was US$1,150 million, about 10 times the value of Kenya's third most valuable export, coffee. Kenya's other significant exports are petroleum products, sold to near neighbors, fish, cement, pyrethrum, and sisal. The leading imports are crude petroleum, chemicals, manufactured goods, machinery, and transportation equipment. Africa is Kenya's largest export market, followed by the European Union.[55]

The major destinations for exports are Uganda, Tanzania, the United Kingdom, and the Netherlands. Major suppliers are China, India, United Arab Emirates, Saudi Arabia, and South Africa. Kenya's main exports to the United States are garments traded under the terms of the African Growth and Opportunity Act (AGOA). Despite AGOA, Kenya's apparel industry is struggling to hold its ground against Asian competition and runs a trade deficit with the United States. Many of Kenya's problems relating to the export of goods are believed by economists to be caused by the fact that Kenya's exports are inexpensive items that do not bring substantial amounts of money into the country.[55]

Kenya is the dominant trade partner for Uganda (12.3% exports, 15.6% imports) and Rwanda (30.5% exports, 17.3% imports).[71][72].

Balance of Trade

Kenya typically has a substantial trade deficit. The trade balance fluctuates widely because Kenya's main exports are primary commodities subject to the effects of both world prices and weather. In 2005 Kenya's income from exports was about US$3.2 billion. The payment for imports was about US$5.7B, yielding a trade deficit of about US$2.5B.[55]

Foreign Investment Policies

Kenyan policies on foreign investment generally have been favorable since independence, with occasional tightening of restrictions to promote the africanisation of enterprises. Foreign investors have been guaranteed ownership and the right to remit dividends, royalties, and capital. In the 1970s, the government disallowed foreign investment unless there was also some government participation in the ownership of an enterprise.[55]

Despite these restrictions, between 60% and 70% of industry is still owned from abroad. A significant portion of this can be traced to fraudulent asset transfers by British colonialists during the transition to independence.[73] This created widespread poverty and encouraged the conditions that would lead to dependency on foreign aid. However, Kenyan has had more economic success and more success raising its own quality of life than many of its neighbors in sub-Saharan Africa.[55]

Agriculture in Kenya

The agricultural sector continues to dominate Kenya's economy, although only 15% of Kenya's total land area has sufficient fertility and rainfall to be farmed, and only 7 or 8% can be classified as first-class land. In 2006, almost 75% of working Kenyans made their living on the land, compared with 80% in 1980. About one-half of total agricultural output is non-marketed subsistence production. Agriculture is the second largest contributor to Kenya's gross domestic product (GDP), after the service sector. In 2005 agriculture, including forestry and fishing, accounted for about 24% of GDP, as well as for 18% of wage employment and 50% of revenue from exports. The principal cash crops are tea, horticultural produce, and coffee; horticultural produce and tea are the main growth sectors and the most valuable of all of Kenya's exports. In 2005 horticulture accounted for 23% and tea for 22% of total export earnings. Coffee has declined in importance with depressed world prices, accounting for just 5% of export receipts in 2005. The production of major food staples such as corn is subject to sharp weather-related fluctuations. Production downturns periodically necessitate food aid—for example, in 2004 aid was needed for 1.8

million people because of Kenya's intermittent droughts. However, the expansion of credit to the agricultural sector has enabled farmers to better deal with the large risk of agriculture based on rainfall and the dramatic fluctuations of the prices of agricultural products.[55]

Tea, coffee, sisal, pyrethrum, corn, and wheat are grown in the fertile highlands, one of the most successful agricultural production regions in Africa. Livestock predominates in the semi-arid savanna to the north and east. Coconuts, pineapples, cashew nuts, cotton, sugarcane, sisal, and corn are grown in the lower-lying areas.[55]

Forestry and Fishing

Resource degradation has reduced output from forestry. In 2004 round wood removals came to 22,162,000 cubic meters. Fisheries are of local importance around Lake Victoria and have potential on Lake Turkana. Kenya's total catch reported in 2004 was 128,000 metric tons. However, output from fishing has been declining because of ecological disruption. Pollution, overfishing, and the use of unauthorized fishing equipment have led to falling catches and have endangered local fish species.[55]

Mining and Minerals

Kenya has no significant mineral endowment. The mining and quarrying sector makes a negligible contribution to the economy, accounting for less than 1% of GDP. The majority of this is contributed by the soda ash operation at Lake Magadi in south-central Kenya. Thanks largely to rising soda ash output, Kenya's mineral production in 2005 reached more than 1 million tons. One of Kenya's largest foreign-investment projects in recent years is the planned expansion of Magadi Soda. Apart from soda ash, the chief minerals produced are limestone, gold, salt, large quantities of niobium, fluorspar, and fossil fuel.[55]

All unextracted minerals are government property, under the Mining Act. The Department of Mines and Geology, under the Ministry of Environment and Natural Resources, controls exploration and exploitation of minerals.[55]

Industry and Manufacturing

Although Kenya is the most industrially developed country in East Africa, manufacturing still accounts for only 14% of GDP. This represents only a slight increase since independence. The rapid expansion of the sector immediately after independence stagnated in the 1980s, hampered by shortages in hydroelectric power, high energy costs, dilapidated transport infrastructure, and the dumping of cheap imports. However, due to urbanization, the industry and manufacturing sectors have become increasingly important to the Kenyan economy, and this has been reflected by an increasing GDP per capita. Industrial activity, concentrated around the three largest urban centers, Nairobi, Mombasa, and Kisumu, is dominated by food-processing industries such as grain milling, beer production, and sugarcane crushing, and the fabrication of consumer goods, e.g., vehicles from kits. Kenya also has an oil refinery that processes imported crude petroleum into petroleum products, mainly for the domestic market. In addition, a substantial and expanding informal sector engages in small-scale manufacturing of household goods, motor-vehicle parts, and farm implements.[55]

Kenya's inclusion among the beneficiaries of the US Government's African Growth and Opportunity Act (AGOA) gave a boost to manufacturing. Since AGOA took effect in 2000, Kenya's clothing sales to the United States increased from US$44 million to US$270M in 2006. Other initiatives to strengthen manufacturing include favorable tax measures, including the removal of duty on capital equipment and other raw materials.[55]

Energy in Kenya

The largest segment of Kenya's electricity supply comes from hydroelectric stations at dams along the upper Tana River, as well as the Turkwel Gorge Dam in the west. A petroleum-fired plant on the coast, geothermal facilities at Olkaria (near Nairobi), and electricity imported from Uganda make up the balance. Kenya's installed capacity stood at 1,142 megawatts a year between 2001 and 2003. The state-owned Kenya Electricity Generating Company (KenGen), established in 1997 under the name Kenya Power Company, handles the generation of electricity, while the Kenya Power and Lighting Company (KPLC)[74] handles transmission and distribution. Shortfalls of electricity occur periodically, when drought reduces water flow. In 1997 and 2000, for example, drought prompted severe power rationing, with economically damaging 12-hour blackouts. Frequent outages and high cost of power remain serious obstacles to economic activity. Tax and other concessions are planned to encourage investment in hydroelectricity and in geothermal energy, in which Kenya is a pioneer. The government plans to open two new power stations in 2008, Sondu Miriu (hydroelectric) and Olkaria IV (geothermal), but power demand growth is strong, and demand is still expected to outpace supply during periods of drought.[55]

Kenya currently imports all crude petroleum requirements, and petroleum accounts for 20% to 25% of the national import bill. Hydrocarbon reserves were recently found in Kenya's semi-arid northern region of Turkana after several decades of intermittent exploration. Offshore prospecting also continues. Kenya Petroleum Refineries, a 50:50 joint venture between the government and several major oil corporations, operates the country's sole oil refinery in Mombasa. The refinery's production is transported via Kenya's Mombasa–Nairobi pipeline.[55] However, the refinery is currently non-operational. In 2004, oil consumption was estimated at 55,000 barrels (8,700 m³) a day.

Tourism

Kenya's services sector, which contributes about 63% of GDP, is dominated by tourism. The tourism sector exhibited steady growth after independence and by the late 1980s had become the country's principal source of foreign exchange. In the late 1990s, a terrorism-related downturn in tourism followed the 1998 bombing of the US Embassy in Nairobi and subsequent negative travel advisories from Western governments. The government of Kenya and tourism industry organizations have taken steps to address security issues and to reverse negative publicity, including establishing a tourist police and launching marketing campaigns in key tourist origin markets.[55]

Tourists are attracted to the coastal beaches and the game reserves, notably the expansive Tsavo East National Park and Tsavo West National Park (20,808 square kilometers) in the southeast. The majority of tourists are from Germany and the United Kingdom. In 2006 tourism generated US$803 million, up from US$699 million the previous year.[55]

Kenya has also contributed to boosting tourism in other countries; the Nairobi-headquartered Serena Hotel is the most consistently high-rated hotel in Pakistan.

Financial Services

Kenya is East Africa's hub for financial services. The Nairobi Stock Exchange (NSE) is ranked 4th in Africa in terms of market capitalization.

The Kenya banking system is supervised by the Central Bank of Kenya. As of late July 2004, the system consisted of 43 commercial banks (down from 48 in 2001), several non-bank financial institutions, including mortgage companies, four savings and loan associations, and many foreign-exchange bureaus. Two of the four largest banks, the Kenya Commercial Bank and the National Bank of Kenya, are partially government-owned, and the others, Barclays Bank and Standard Chartered, are majority foreign-owned. Most of the smaller banks are family-owned and -operated.[55]

Labor

In 2006, Kenya's labor force was estimated to include about 12 million workers, almost 75% in agriculture. The number employed outside small-scale agriculture and pastoralism was about 6 million. In 2004, about 15% of the labor force was officially classified as unemployed. Other estimates place Kenya's unemployment much higher, in some estimates up to 40%. In recent years, Kenya's labor force has shifted from the countryside to the cities, such as Nairobi, as Kenya becomes increasingly urbanized.[55]

The labor force participation rate in Kenya has been constant from 1997 to 2010 for both women and men. In 1997, 65% of women were employed in some type of labor and 76% of men were employed.[75] In 2005, 60% of women and 70% of men were in the labor force, increasing slightly to 61% of women and 72% of men in 2010.[75]

Family Farm Labor

In the past 20 years, Kenyans have moved away from family farming towards jobs that pay wages or to start small businesses outside of agriculture.[76] In 1989, 4.5 million Kenyans out of a total working population of 7.3M worked on family farms.[76] In 2009, only 6.5M Kenyans out of a total working population of 14.3M worked on family farms.[76] Of these, 3.8M were women and 2.7M were men.[76]

Wage-Job Labor

According to the World Bank 2012 Kenya Economic Update, "Men are much more likely than women to hold wage jobs, and women are more likely to work on family farms. Twice as many men as women hold wage jobs, and more men work principally in wage jobs than on family farms. Most Kenyans are now striving to get modern, wage jobs." Modern wage jobs include being an "engineer, telecommunication specialist, cut flower worker, teacher, construction worker, housekeepers, professionals, any industrial and manufacturing job, and port and dock workers."[76] In 1989, there were only 1.9M Kenyans employed in wage work.[76] In 2009 this number had increased to 5.1M. In 2009, 3.4M men and 1.3M women were employed in wage jobs.[76]

Non-farm self-employment/"Jua Kali"

In Kenya, the "Jua Kali" sector is another name for the informal economy, also described as non-farming self-employment.[76] Jua Kali is Swahili for "hot sun" and refers to the idea that the workers in the informal economy work under the fierce sun.[77] The informal sector consists of self-employment and wage employment that are neither regulated by the Kenyan government nor recognized for legal protection. As a result, informal sector employment does not contribute to Kenya's GDP.[77] Non-farm self-employment has risen from 1989 to 2009.

The World Bank characterizes non-farm self-employment to include jobs such as "street vendor, shop owner, dressmaker, assistant, fishmonger, caterer, etc." [76] Non-farm self-employment has risen from a total of 0.9M in 1989 to a total of 2.7M in 2009.[76] Men make up 1.4M workers, and women workers number 1.3M.[76]

As of 2009, Kenya's informal economy accounts for about 80% of the total employment for the country. Most informal workers are self-employed, with few entrepreneurs who employ others. The informal sector contributes economic activity equal to 35% of the total GDP in Kenya, provides an informal finance structure in the shape of the rotating savings and credit associations (ROSCAs), and provides an income for those with lower socioeconomic status.[77]

The drawbacks of the informal economy are that it promotes smuggling and tax evasion, and lacks social protection. Most members of the informal sector have low educational attainment but are responsible for developing all of their own skilled labor through apprenticeships. Many choose to enter the informal economy due to the lack of fees, shorter training sessions, and the availability of practical content that is largely absent from formal education. The rising cost of education and lack of guarantees of future employment have caused many workers to transfer to informal apprenticeships.[78]

The Impact of Customary Law on the Informal Economy

Customary law has some adverse impacts on women in the informal sector.[79] Although the Law of Succession Act (Chapter 160 of 2010 and revised 2012) of the Laws of Kenya gives equality in distribution of intestate properties, the effects are yet to be realized as the implementation of this act is slow among some communities. Some of the inequalities and discriminations against women are as follows. The British 1882 Married Women's Property Act gives married women equal property rights and the Law of Succession Act gives women inheritance rights, but the constitution exempts those who are considered "members of a particular race or tribe" from being governed by these laws, and instead allows customary law to remain in practice.[79] Customary law allows for discrimination against women and keeps them from accessing assets, land, and property that might otherwise allow them to have collateral for business finance. This restricts the amount of credit that women entrepreneurs might otherwise use to enter either the formal or informal sector. Some examples of discriminatory statutes in the constitution are the Law of Succession Act, the Divorce Laws, and the Children's Act 2001.[79] The overall result is that unmarried women inherit less than their brothers, married women are not expected to receive any inheritance, and a woman only has permission to manage her husband's property as a surrogate for her sons. Women without children are still omitted from inheritance on the death of their husband.[79] Because women have fewer assets and low educational attainment, women are more likely to turn to the informal economy than men.

Challenges

The economy's heavy dependence on rain-fed agriculture and the tourism sector leaves it vulnerable to cycles of boom and bust. The agricultural sector employs nearly 75% of the country's 52 million people. Half of the sector's output remains subsistence production.[55]

Kenya's economic performance has been hampered by numerous factors: heavy dependence on a few agricultural exports that are vulnerable to world price fluctuations, population growth that has outstripped economic growth, prolonged drought that has necessitated power rationing, deteriorating infrastructure, and extreme disparities of wealth that have limited the opportunities of most to develop their skills and knowledge. Poor governance and corruption also have had a negative impact on growth, making it expensive to do business in Kenya.[80] According to

Transparency International, Kenya ranks among the world's six most corrupt countries. Bribery and fraud cost Kenya as much as US$1 billion a year. Kenyans pay some 16 bribes a month, for two in every three encounters with public officials, even though 23% of them live on less than US$1 per day. Another large drag on Kenya's economy is the burden of HIV/AIDS.[55]

Despite the above challenges, let us look at Kenya's economic outlook as we move to 2020. Kenya's economy grew 5.1 percent in quarter three of 2019, a drop from 6.4 percent in the same period in 2018. The drop is likely to further put pressure on the economy at a time when Kenyans feel 2019 was a bad year. The Kenya National Bureau of Statistics (KNBS) gave the report on Tuesday, saying the deceleration in growth was mainly on account of suppressed growth in most of the sectors of the economy.[7]

The slowed overall performance, according to KNBS, was occasioned by relatively slower growths in activities of manufacturing (3.1 percent), electricity and water supply (4.9 percent), construction (6.6 percent), wholesale and retail trade (4.7 percent) and transportation and storage (7.1 percent), relative to notable performances recorded in the same quarter of 2018.

Inflation Rises

The KNBS also reported that inflation rose for the fourth consecutive month to close the year at 5.82 percent in December, eating into the purchasing power of consumers. The rise was from 5.56 percent recorded in November, 4.95 percent in October and 3.83 percent in September, which was the lowest rate in 2019.

---

[7] https://www.theeastafrican.co.ke/business/Kenya-economic-growth-rate-drops/2560-5403744-9vettuz/index.html.

At 5.82 percent, inflation is still within the government's target of between 5 and 7.5 percent, but the sharp rise in the last quarter points to tough times ahead. KNBS attributes the rise in inflation, which measures the cost of living, to a rise in the prices of some food and non-alcoholic drinks. Households are bracing for New Year blues as the prices of commonly purchased items shot up, significantly weakening their purchasing power.

Further, households, which generally spend more on food items and fares during the festive season, face additional expenses such as tuition fees at the start of January as schools open.

Food Prices

The KNBS report shows the food and non-alcohol drinks index increased by 1.46 percent at the height of December festivities.

"A high increase of vegetables was recorded despite the heavy rains. For instance, the price of kale, popularly known as sukuma wiki, tomatoes, spinach and onions increased by 5.6 percent, 7.8 percent, 9.1 percent and 5.1 percent respectively compared with prices for the previous month," it states. Already, the price of milled maize flour has hit unprecedented levels with a 2kg packet, overtaking wheat to retail at Sh135. This price increased in December by 0.77 percent on the month–on–month inflation and by 52.26 percent, compared to same period in 2018.

Other Prices

The prices of other items such as beans, beef and sugar increased by 1.51 percent, 1.11 percent and 4.12 percent respectively. KNBS says a kilogram of beans is now retailing at Sh124.95 compared to Sh123 in November and Sh107.6 in December 2018. However, during the same period, prices of unpacketed fresh milk and mangoes dropped by 0.67 percent and 3.44 percent respectively.

A liter of fresh unpacked milk now costs Sh64.16, a small drop from Sh64.59in November but more expensive than the Sh60.69 at a similar period in 2018.

Petrol, Electricity

According to the KNBS, the government clampdown on charcoal trade wiped out savings from downward review of petroleum prices by the energy regulator as the housing, water electricity, gas and other fuel index increased marginally between November and December.

"Despite a decrease in pump prices of diesel and petrol during the month, the transport index increased by 2.1 percent mainly as a result of increase in transport fares," it said.

However, consumers had a reprieve in the cost of electricity following declines of 3.25 percent and 2.26 percent per 50 kWh and 200 kWh respectively from November.

CONCLUSION

In conclusion, the option for developing countries to address the changing employment scenario is the strengthening of sustainable community-owned enterprises through use of technological advancement.

CHAPTER 3

INITIAL DEVELOPMENTS OF MODERN KENYA AND SUSTAINABILITY

Many of us remember the 1960s especially after Kenya gained independence from the British. It was a period when a lot of aggressive moves designed to increase various capacities to manage Kenya under an African administration were undertaken. These included moves to transfer the White Highlands to Kenyans, to transfer businesses to indigenous people (this saw the establishment of the Kenyanization Bureau), to increase educational institutions to provide required manpower, to increase hospitals and medical staff, and to fully transfer British administration and the economy to Kenyans to avoid what Mwalimu Julius Nyerere once termed as "Uhuru wa Bendera" (so that independence may not be a change of national flags—from the Union Jack to the Kenyan National flag).

This was the time of the white settlers, not sure what Kenyan independence had in store for them, opted to sell their land to the new Kenyan government or to the new African settlers. I call them new African settlers because the land that the new owners bought courtesy of funding from the Settlement Fund Trustees was expansive compared to what they previously owned. Some of the land bought from British settlers by the government was meant to settle landless Kenyans. However, Kenya did not have enough personnel to do all the adjudication required.

In the early 1960s, there was a growing feeling among many young Americans that they should do something to help the world, and in response, President John F. Kennedy established the American Peace Corps in 1961. This saw many Americans with skills in different areas going to serve in many parts of the world as Peace Corps volunteers.

THE PEACE CORPS

> The Peace Corps sends Americans with a passion for service abroad on behalf of the United States to work with communities and create lasting change. Volunteers develop sustainable solutions to address challenges in education, health, community economic development, agriculture, the environment, and youth development. Through their Peace Corps experience, volunteers gain a unique cultural understanding and a life-long commitment to service that positions them to succeed in today's global economy. Since President John F. Kennedy established the Peace Corps in 1961, more than 235,000 Americans of all ages have served in 141 countries worldwide.[8]

Many Peace Corps volunteers came to Kenya, and today, places like Uasin Gishu/Kapsabet, Elgeyo Marakwet, Nakuru, and Kericho are grateful for the work done by these volunteers to allocate them the landholdings they have.

The primary goals of the post-independence Kenyan African administration were to eradicate poverty, disease, and ignorance by increasing literacy levels, increasing jobs, and improving health care of Kenyans. At the time of independence, there were very few secondary schools in the country; the few that existed were sponsored by religious organizations such as the Catholic Church, African Inland Mission, or an alliance of several religions such as Alliance High

---

[8] This is according to the Peace Corps website.

School. Such schools did not want to hand over control of their schools to the government.

To increase the number of students receiving a Cambridge General Certificate of Education, a Cambridge Higher School Certificate, or a London General Certificate of Education, more schools were required. As a result, Harambee Secondary Schools started mushrooming all over the country. These were secondary schools initiated with funding from the local people that after successful performance over a period of years would gradually start receiving government-funded teachers and ultimately become government-sponsored schools.

A big influx of Peace Corps volunteers helped fill Kenya's need for teachers of English, math, chemistry, and physics. Other Peace Corps volunteers provided support to the agricultural sector at the ministry level and in the field at Agriculture Development Corporation (ADC) farms that promoted the breeding of dairy and beef cattle. The Peace Corps provided much support to such Kenyan institutions until the country developed its own qualified personnel to serve in these sectors.

Other aid agencies were instrumental in building up the government's capabilities. The key partner at the Ministry of Cooperative Development since independence has been the Nordic Cooperative Project. The project funded the establishment of the Cooperative College of Kenya as well as seconding Nordic Cooperative Officers in the Ministry of Cooperative Development to work with corresponding government officers. Let us look at this in more details.

NORDIC ASSISTANCE TO THE COOPERATIVE SECTOR—AN EXAMPLE OF SUSTAINABLE DONOR INTERVENTION

My first job before joining college was with the Department of Cooperative Development, and I wondered why we had some foreigners working in the department. I was told that these were Nordic Cooperative officers who were working with Kenyan counterparts to train them in various aspects of the management of cooperative organizations. My boss informed me that there was an agreement between the Kenyan government and the Nordic countries to provide training and develop the capacities of Kenyans to run cooperative organizations. The areas of support included the following.

- At a national level, to provide funding to construct and operate a cooperative college for advanced training in cooperative principles and management for cooperative personnel and leaders. In this respect, the Nordic Cooperative Project established the Cooperative College of Kenya to design, develop, and implement cooperative education and training program in administrative and management skills in Kenya.
- At a provincial level, to establish and operationalize provincial cooperative training centers to provide short courses for personnel and leaders as well as for the coordination of member education activities.
- To build the capacities of the Department of Cooperative Development staff, the Nordic Cooperative Project was to station advisors at the department headquarters and at provincial and district levels to train Kenyans on improved management of cooperative organizations.
- The Nordic Cooperative Project was to provide support to the Department of Cooperative Development in planning of cooperative development in marketing, savings, and credit cooperatives that had started mushrooming in various parts of Kenya.

After attaining independence from the British in 1963, Kenya experienced an increase in small-scale coffee production and in farmers registering coffee-marketing cooperatives to process the coffee beans from grading, dehulling, and drying the beans before marketing the dried coffee beans through the Coffee Board of Kenya. The management of these new cooperatives required management, accounting, and financial control systems to ensure benefits to the members; hence the importance of the Nordic Cooperative Project.

These young cooperative societies needed support also in the area of production credit, which small-scale coffee producers had no access to. The source of credit ideally would have been the Cooperative Bank of Kenya (established in 1965), but as did other banks, it required collateral to provide credit to small-scale coffee farmers. The Nordic Cooperative Program worked with the Department of Cooperative Department and the Cooperative Bank to set up the Cooperative

Production Credit Scheme and the Cooperative Savings Scheme (CPCS). This scheme called for a system of hypothecation of coffee sales as a guarantee to provide credit to coffee cooperatives to ensure a successful CPCS. The system was designed to ensure that the Coffee Board of Kenya disbursed coffee sales only through the Cooperative Bank to facilitate recovery of any credit or cash advances to coffee cooperatives.

Once the loan proceeds were released to the coffee cooperatives, individual farmers got their respective input credit and as well as advances on the crops they would grow. To ensure efficient running of this credit management, accounting and financial control systems were installed and implemented by the Nordic Cooperative advisors, who worked alongside cooperative officers and trained cooperative movement staff at district cooperative unions to ensure credit disbursement and recovery from individual farmers.

The coffee-production and -marketing cooperatives benefitted a lot from the Nordic Cooperative Project especially in the area of management, accounting, and financial control systems. Equally, the Cooperative Bank benefitted from the loan recovery systems.

One other area worthy of mention to which the Nordic Cooperative Project provided support was in sugar production and marketing in the Nyanza area of Kenya. The major donor in the sugar industry was the World Bank through the Integrated Development Agricultural Program (IADP I & II) disbursed through the Cooperative Bank of Kenya, but the management, accounting, and financial control systems were designed and implemented by the Nordic Cooperative Project and cooperative officers of the Department of Cooperative Development. (The sugar industry in Kenya under small-scale producers has never been a success, but that is the subject of another chapter.)

An important sector in which the Nordic Cooperative Project had a big impact is the savings and credit cooperatives, the precursors of the modern-day Savings and Credit Cooperatives (SACCOs). The Nordic Cooperative Project came up with the initial management, accounting, and financial control systems for such cooperatives. According to the African Report Daily Newsletter, the SACCO sector embraces more than 10 million savers and collectively controls savings of $4.5 billion and an asset base of $6.2 billion. It employs half a million people, and in 2017, it contributed 5.72 percent of Kenya's nominal GDP.

Unlike corporate directors of a private enterprise, many directors of cooperative organizations do not prioritize corporate profits but assume their roles as distributors of benefits to the membership to earn reelection. This conflict of interests tends to subjugate the profit-making objective of the organization and attract board members attuned to political survival rather than good management.

Consequently, the impact of the Nordic Cooperative Project is not well registered in the cooperative movement because of the governance of the institutions. The governance by members seeking to satisfy their electoral constituency brought to the management boards of the cooperative movement of the Kenya National Federation of Cooperatives (KNFC) and the Kenya Union of Savings and Credit Cooperatives (KUSCCO) directors whose profit motive for the organization was secondary. Therefore, the two apex organizations of the cooperative movement in Kenya have not and are not likely to grow financially into the giants they ought to be.

CHAPTER 4

HOW THE SUGAR INDUSTRY IN KENYA HAS PROVED UNSUSTAINABLE

In an effort to distribute income to the rural population after independence in 1963, the Kenyan government settled people in parts of Western and Nyanza Provinces to start small-scale sugar production organized under the cooperative movement. Consequently, officers from the Department of Cooperative Development were deployed to help groups of farmers develop production and marketing cooperatives. These cooperatives structures would be conduits of a World Bank funding program (IADP—Integrated Agricultural Development Project I & II) channeled through the Cooperative Bank of Kenya.

Similarly, a sugar research station was established at Kibos in Nyanza to conduct research and development for sugarcane farming in those provinces. The center developed and recommended high-sucrose sugarcane for farmers. The government deployed cooperative officers to those provinces to ensure that the farmer groups were registered as cooperatives as required by law so they could access loans to grow and market sugarcane. Most of the initial cooperative officers hailed from those two provinces to ensure that the local population was served by their own and to ensure the success of the sugar industry. Loan money was disbursed by the Cooperative Bank to the district cooperative unions for disbursement to individual cooperative societies and the farmers.

By ensuring that all was in place, the government hoped the small-scale schemes would give farmers a cash crop that would lift them out of poverty by making them stakeholders in the multibillion-dollar sugar industry.

However, the government's and the farmers' dream was never realized. The IADP credit, channeled through the Cooperative Bank of Kenya to develop the sugar industry, was never paid back. The failure to develop the sugar industry and the credit scheme had many reasons including the following.

- After Kenya achieved independence, the project was mooted in the 1960s and '70s by politicians who wanted to settle peasants on land previously owned by the British settlers.
- Sugar production modeled on small-scale grower schemes had never worked in other countries. While other sugarcane growing countries (Zambia, Malawi, Sudan) retained colonial-era sugar plantations, Kenya went for the more politically correct, more expensive, smallholder schemes as bureaucrats struggled to settle the landless and allow farmers to grow new cash crops, but technocrats at the Ministry of Agriculture and Cooperative Development decided to go ahead because the experiment of small-scale grower schemes as these made political sense.
- Sugar production required sugarcane to be grown, harvested, and delivered to the mills with almost split-second timing day after day, week after week, but it became clear that that was impossible to do as it was difficult to maintain the same standards for each farmer.

   Plantation sugar planting had succeeded in neighboring countries as management ensured all cane was grown, harvested, and delivered to the mill at the appointed times. Employees who did not comply were disciplined according to the terms of their employment. Under small-scale outgrower production, it was not possible to instill the same discipline in small-scale growers.
- Chemelil, which started operations in 1965, was the first to experiment with smallholder sugar production in Kenya, and within six years,

officials knew it was a failure. It became obvious that small-scale sugar production was a failure, but the government continued pumping money into small-scale production of sugar. Even today, sugar farmers are generally impoverished.

According to the *Scientific Research Journal*[9]), sugarcane production in Kenya has declined due to several challenges. Mumias, so far the largest miller in Kenya with about 66,000 registered growers, is producing at only 20 percent of its capacity as it struggles with a biting sugarcane shortage.

At the farm level, sugar productivity is low due to poor seed of long-maturing varieties, smut disease, high costs of input, and delayed payments to farmers. Sugarcane in western Kenya takes eighteen to twenty-four months to grow to maturity while Sudan is able to harvest its varieties of cane within fourteen months. As well, sugar production costs have increased from about $676 per ton in 2014 to $1,007 per ton in 2018. This compares poorly with production costs of $350 per ton in Malawi and $400 per ton in Zambia.

The sugar industry is unsustainable at the country level; Kenya continues to import sugar from neighboring countries and continues to subsidize small-scale farmers and sugar millers without any meaningful change from one year to the next. At the small-scale farmer level, poverty continues to bite the farmers, who are disillusioned by the poor proceeds from sugarcane sales.

RELICS OF UNSUSTAINABLE DEVELOPMENT

Maintenance refers to the work need to keep something in its proper condition. Preventive maintenance keeps it in good repair while corrective maintenance fixes it when it breaks down. Both cost money of course that has to be set aside or borrowed.

Most tribal languages in Kenya have words for *repair* and *replace* but not for *maintenance*; the concept of maintenance is foreign to them, and that affects not just the machinery they use but also roads and other infrastructure.

When you visit most of the district headquarters in Kenya, you will see

---

[9] *Scientific Research Journal* 10, no. 11 (November 2019).

abandoned construction camps and graveyards of rusted earthmoving equipment. The massive machines— Caterpillar front loaders, Kumatsu road graders, bulldozers—look as if they had died young; some still had all their "teeth." You see derelict equipment and vehicles, usually Land Rovers, almost everywhere in the district commissioner's (DC's) yard that have suffered not from years of use but from lack of maintenance and parts. These mute orphans of development had long been forgotten, written off by their donors' accountants in Washington, London, and elsewhere.

CHAPTER 5

THE CASE OF SUSTAINABILITY IN RURAL WATER SYSTEMS

HOW THE NEW SETTLERS OF NGORIKA IMPLEMENTED A SUSTAINABLE WATER PROJECT

Kenya has suffered water shortages especially in Nairobi and in some rural areas, but the Ngorika Water Project in Nyandarua District of Central Kenya is a model water project whose design, implementation, and management is worth emulating. Let us look at what makes this project stand out as a model for other water supply programs.

The Ngorika Water Project is in the Ngorika sublocation of Dundori Division of Nyandarua District. This area was part of the colonial White Highlands, land owned by a British settler. In 1970, the Kenyan government bought it and settled some landless people from parts of the colonial native reserves in Central Province in the 1970s. Ngorika sublocation thus became Ngorika Settlement.

A little background on these new settlers is necessary for us to appreciate their pressing need for a sustainable water supply.

The White Highlands were prime lands in Kenya that the colonial government allocated to white settlers mainly as a reward for serving in the

British army during World War I. The land in question was equivalent to three million hectares of which over half was high-potential arable land suitable for cash crop farming—coffee, tea and sugar—and dairy and large-scale livestock farming. There were over 3,600 farms ranging from 400 to over 800 hectares although in the large-scale livestock farming, some of the landholdings were more than 20,000 hectares.

The White Highlands constituted about 21,000 of Kenya's 356,000 square-kilometer area, a substantial landholding by a small European population on 3,600 farms; 68 percent of Kenya's land is remote and unsuited to farming. The White Highlands occupied 6 percent of the remaining 32 percent of arable land while the remaining 26 percent of the land was shared by about six million Africans, the native reserves.

These reserves occupied about 84,000 square kilometers. Each of the reserves was for the use of a particular ethnic group. The administration established firm social-political boundaries between the reserves and succeeded in preventing social-political interactions between the reserves and therefore prevented interethnic political relations. This solidified ethnic identities and was the cause of the tribal woes that bedeviled the integration of Kenya as one nation and caused bottlenecks in the development of modern Kenya.

The new settlers in Ngorika were hardworking people wishing to undertake dairy and horticultural farming activities to raise their standard of living. The potential for commercial dairy and horticultural farming existed, but the lack of a sustainable water supply for human consumption, irrigation, and dairy cattle was a major constraint. Water in the area came from two springs and a river flowing through Ngorika. How did the new settlers get a self-sustaining water project implemented in Ngorika?

The Kenyan government through the district water engineer surveyed the potential for increasing and distributing water resources in the area. Three sources of water were identified that if harnessed would satisfy the Ngorika community's needs. The Ngorika Water Project was presented to the District Development Committee (DDC) for approval and funding. The DDC approved the project but was able to get European Union funding only to the level of KES (Kenya shilling) 1,500,000, far below what would be required to develop all that was needed to develop and manage a sustainable water supply.

The Ngorika community approached Technoserve to set up management systems, to source funding for the project, to implement and manage it, to train staff and management committees to manage the project, and to eventually hand it over to the community. I was appointed the leader of the team to implement the project. Some of the strategies we set out to implement included these.

- Design of water users' bylaws and registration of the Ngorika Water Project as a legal entity registered under the Office of the President. It was necessary to work with the elected leaders of the proposed water project to approve bylaws for the project. Some of the key principles included in the bylaws addressed the rights and duties of members and the election, duties, and responsibilities of the management committee members among other considerations. Equally important was a system that would require users to meter and pay monthly for their water usage.
- Design of management, accounting, and financial control systems for the water project. It was important to design a system that could track members' deposits and water usage fees and the wages and salaries of the project's staff.
- Hire and train staff to manage the project.
- Work with the committee to mobilize members to dig trenches for distribution pipes.
- Train the committee and staff on management of the project.

Work started in 1986. The agreement between the community and Technoserve was that the villagers were to contribute a day's labor out of every five working days. Without any mechanical equipment, they were going to dig all the trenches and lay the pipe.

Technoserve agreed to source funds for the project and the technical assistance costs, but that took time, and the local administration got anxious and accused Technoserve of using the community to raise money for its own needs. Another complaint was that livestock could fall into the trenches being dug.

The local DC asked me what we were doing at the project, and I told him that we had identified a donor to fund the project. He insisted that we remit the money for procurement of piping and other materials to the district treasury.

Work stopped; our mandate from the donor was that we ensure all materials were procured transparently. Our fight with the district administration was resolved only when a high-ranking officer from Office of the President intervened and gave us permission to continue working within our donor's requirements.

One lesson we learned was the importance of procuring all materials on a competitive basis rather than funneling capital development costs through any intermediaries because some intermediaries do not have reporting responsibilities to the donor and may not allow the donor to audit the use of the funds.

The water project was completed with donor funds from the Church of Latter-Day Saints (Mormon Church of the USA), and in March 1989, the Ngorika Water Project was officially opened at a function attended by senior government officials from Central Province and Nairobi.

At the official commissioning of the project, a notable beneficiary testified that she used to walk eight miles each way to draw water for her family. She testified that it was a dream to see water flowing from a faucet outside her house. She said that the time she saved by being able to draw water from it would be used to grow horticultural products and manage dairy operations.

CHAPTER 6

A SUSTAINABLE COMMUNITY-OWNED ENTERPRISE

ENGINEER CHEESE COMPANY

Engineer Cheese Company is a prototype mala milk [10] community organization that the author worked with in the late 1980s. It is a good example of a community-owned enterprise whose systems can be replicated at various production levels.

Many parts of Kenya have poor road communication and no electricity. Dairy farmers in these areas are often not able to get the milk their cows produce in the evening to the nearest cooling plant before it spoils. This evening milk represents nearly half the milk produced daily, and having it rejected is expensive for dairy farmers. A solution for this problem was to process this milk into a cultured or fermented form in small-scale plants close to the farmers.

Cultured milk has many advantages over fresh pasteurized milk in this situation. It can be processed without electricity or a power source apart from a wood-burning boiler. The milk will keep in a safe and palatable form for at least five days without refrigeration. The process was thoroughly tested, and

---

[10] Mala milk is fermented milk.

such cultured milk has been successfully marketed as mala milk by the Kenya Co-operative Creameries (KCC). The fact that fermenting milk is a traditional method of preserving milk in Kenya accounts for its ready market acceptance.

Our experience in the past year with Naishi Enterprises, a mala milk processing plant in Nakuru District, has proven that small-scale production and marketing of mala milk is technically feasible and commercially viable. The demand for mala milk produced at Naishi is currently outstripping production. Market tests at Naivasha, the target market for mala milk from the Engineer Cheese Company, have uncovered a potentially good market.

The following report examines the feasibility of a small cultured milk plant producing five hundred liters per day that would be established in Kinangop, where there is unmarketed surplus evening milk. The description and business plan refer specifically to Engineer Cheese Company, but they can be replicated in other areas where surplus milk and a potential market exist.

THE PROCESS AND THE MARKET

To make cultured milk on a small envisaged involves the following basic steps and processes.

1. Farmers would deliver milk to the plant and be paid by weight and for at least the equivalent of the KCC (Brookside) farm gate price. Payment will be as quick as possible and preferably daily to ensure regular supplies.
2. Milk purchases will be tested to ensure freshness and to identify watered-down milk.
3. The milk is then placed in the processing vat, heated to the proper temperature for thirty minutes, and allowed to cool.
4. The starter culture is introduced, and the milk ferments; the milk is ready for marketing the next day.
5. Depending on the nature of the market, the plant can sell the cultured milk packaged or unpackaged. It is preferable that it be sold by the plant to individuals or to wholesalers who would then retail the milk. In this case, it is assumed that the milk is sold in an urban center packaged in half-liter plastic bags.

(An important part of the cultured milk production process is the maintenance of the starter culture. A suitable culture has been developed at the University of Nairobi and is available for a nominal charge.)

Naivasha Town was the main target market for mala milk produced by the Engineer Cheese Company. Naivasha Town is linked to Engineer Town, where the mala plant would be located, by an all-weather, twenty-five-kilometer road.

Naivasha Town was supplied with between 400 and 450 liters of the milk on average four times a week. Sources at the KCC distributor indicated that the mala milk sold out the day it arrived. A brief survey of the mala milk market indicated that there was unmet demand for the product. Consumers have shown a preference for the milk, which they said tasted better and was a full-fat product. Similar preferences had been noted among customers in Gilgil, another market for the milk.

Although we could not quantify the exact mala milk market at Naivasha and Gilgil, we were confident that Engineer Cheese mala milk would find a ready market due to the following.

- Naivasha was a relatively dry region that did not produce enough milk for its consumption needs.
- Supplies of the milk from the KCC were irregular and insufficient.
- The quality of Engineer Cheese mala milk made it capable of outselling other brands.

PROJECT DESCRIPTION

The Mwireri Self-Help Group is an association of 148 dairy farmers who registered their group in 1983. The group is in North Kinangop near a small town called Engineer. Dairy farming is the main economic activity generating more than 70 percent of farmers' income in the region.

The group was formed for the sole purpose of transporting members' and nonmembers' milk. It transports milk for its 148 members at KES 0.30 per kg and KES 0.40 per kg for nonmembers. Fifty-two nonmembers participate in the transport scheme. The group's three lorries transported 2,470 tons of milk for the year ending August 1987.

A survey of evening milk availability among twenty members picked randomly produced this information.

Evening milk available (kg)	Milk Point	Number of Members (f)	Amount
0–10	5	5	25
11–20	15	10	150
21–30	25	4	100
31–40	35	4	140
Total		23	415

Average = 18.04 kg per member

Allowing for the small number of the sample population, we can conclude that an average of eighteen kilograms of evening milk would be available from each member daily; that ensures a supply. The survey also reveals that the above quantities of evening milk currently go to waste. The group has therefore proposed to embark on a scheme to process evening milk initially into mala and if feasible expand to cheese production in due course.

CAPITAL OUTLAY

Projected Capital Expenditure KES 230,000
Equity from Mwireri Group Members KES 130,000
Loan KES 100,000 KES 230,000[11]

It is assumed the capital requirements will be KES 210,000 and working capital KES 20,000.

---

[11] This is the total investment; the group's contribution (equity) is KES 130,000 and a loan KES 100,000.

CAPITAL REQUIREMENTS

Capital Equipment and Costs

- Building: An appropriate building would be constructed by Mwireri Self-Help Group at an estimated cost of KES 80,000 and rented to the Engineer Cheese Company.
- Water tank: A corrugated iron water tank holding 2,000 liters would sit on a simple wooden platform with basic inlet and outlet fittings. Estimated cost KES 5,200. This would be part of that building.
- Processing vat: This is a water bath designed to fit fifty-liter milk churns mounted on a small wood-burning stove that is locally manufactured. Estimated cost KES 18,000.
- Milk cans: Up to twenty fifty-liter standard milk churns for holding cultured milk and for reception of the milk. Estimated cost KES 1,100 each, total KES 22,000. Cans will be bought only as justified by sales and production but are assumed to be all bought at startup.
- Plastic bag sealing equipment: It is assumed that all output of the plant would be retailed in Naivasha, Gilgil, and Nakuru in half-liter plastic bags. In this case, the packaging equipment is situated where no electricity is available. The estimated cost of equipment including two sealing machines, three solar panels, two batteries, and an inverter has been quoted at KES 41,000.
- Lifting equipment: Estimated cost KES 5,000.
- Fridge: To store frozen culture; KES 15,000.
- Quality control equipment and laboratory materials: Required to test the quality of milk delivered and to maintain and prepare the starter culture. Estimated cost KES 20,000.
- Weighing scale: An appropriate scale to weigh milk delivered to the plant; estimated cost KES 7,000.
- Miscellaneous equipment: Including filters, stirrers for cans, thermometers, volume measures, etc. Estimated cost KES 3,400.
- Transport crates: fifty fifty-liter containers to transport (twenty by half-liter) milk pouches; estimate cost KES 7,200.

- Office equipment and furniture: Including chairs, desk, shelving, cash safe, calculator, etc. Estimated cost KES 10,000.
- Contingency: A contingency of 20 percent is added to the estimate for all capital equipment.

With the 20 percent contingency, this totals KES 178,320.

Development Capital Required

- Company registration: Estimated at KES 15,000
- Initial marketing expenses: Provision for introducing the product to wholesalers and retailers, contracting wholesalers, free samples, etc.; estimated KES 15,000.
- Training: Training of manager and production supervisor at Kabete, University of Nairobi. Tuition fees and accommodation are estimated at KES 5,000.
- Design and production of printing plates for milk packages: estimated at KES 700.

Total: KES 30,700.

Stock

The only stocks of significance that will be maintained are of plastic bags; 50,000 are required to ensure against erratic supply due to minimum printing runs.
Total cost: 50,000 times KES 0.20, KES 10,000.

Working Capital

It is estimated that Engineer Cheese will maintain working capital of KES 10,000.

SUMMARY OF CAPITAL REQUIREMENTS

- Capital equipment: KES 178,320
- Development capital: KES 30,700
- Stock: KES 10,000.
- Working capital: 10,000.

Total: KES 229,020.

ASSUMPTIONS FOR THE INCOME AND EXPENDITURE PROJECTIONS

Income

1. Sales of Milk

   Price: The Kenya Cooperative Creameries (KCC) sales price for their mala milk is KES 3 per half-liter. It is expected that packaged cultured milk can be retailed for the same price (i.e., KES 6 per liter) as there appears to be a large unmet demand. In addition, the cultured milk can be labeled as full-fat milk while KCC products are reduced to 2.3 percent fat content. A sales margin of KES 0.75 is assumed; therefore, the packaged milk would be sold wholesale for KES 5.25 per liter. The option exists to market quarter-liter packets at a higher margin but is not included in these projections.

   Volume: The volume purchased will be restricted to evening milk, which is sufficient for the plant capacity. It is then assumed that production volume is dictated by the quality of mala milk that can be marketed until full capacity is achieved. It is assumed that the market will be developed slowly at the following rates.

Month	One-Day Average	
1	50	One-day average
2	100	One-day average
3	200	One-day average
4	400	One-day average
5	500	One-day average
6	500	One day average

Expenditure Assumptions

1. Variable Expenses
   Milk Purchase: Current net payment to farmers

	Members (64)	Nonmembers
Dry season (after transport, cess[12] and capital levy)	KES 2.64	KES 2.44
Rainy season (after transport, cess, and capital levy)	KES 3.12	KES 2.92

(Dry season: May to December;
Rainy season: January to April

The above price structures would be adopted.

    a. Wastage: Spoiled milk and milk that cannot be cultured due to the presence of antibiotics is estimated at 3 percent of milk purchases, equivalent to KES 0.17 per liter of milk valued at the sales price of KES 5.25.

    b. Starter Culture: Starter culture for making cultured milk is available from the University of Nairobi and can be maintained at the processing plant. The cost is estimated at KES 10 per 1,000 liters of milk or KES 0.01 per liter.

---

[12] Cess is a levy or a tax by the local authorities.

    c. Firewood: Firewood is required to fire the processing vat; it is estimated that a normal requirement would be 500 kg of firewood per 1,000 liters of milk, KES 0.10 per liter.

    d. Water: One liter of water is required per liter of milk processed while cooling water is recycled. Piped water is available and currently for free at the Kingangop site.

    e. Detergents and Disinfectants: Detergents and disinfectants are estimated to cost KES 20 per 1,000 liters of milk, KES 0.02 per liter.

    f. Chemicals for Quality Control: These chemicals are estimated to cost KES 15 per 1,000 liters of milk or KES 0.015 per liter of milk.

    g. Packaging: Each plastic bag costs KES 0.40 per liter.

    h. Transport: Transport costs are based on the current cost to the group delivering milk to the KCC, KES 0.30 per liter, the rate charged to fully paid members.

    i. A cess is paid to the Dairy Board equivalent to KES 0.02 per liter of milk processed.

2. Fixed Expenses

    a. Salaries and wages

        i. Production supervisor: KES 1,000 per month for the first six months and KES 1,200 thereafter.

        ii. Two assistant production technicians: KES 700 for the first six months per each for the first six months and thereafter.

        iii. Watchman at KES: 500 for the first six months per month and thereafter.

Total KES 2,900 per month.

    b. Personnel Expenses: Expenses include social security, insurance, medical, uniforms, etc., estimated at 20 percent of salaries and wages, KES 580 per month.

    c. Office Expenses: Allowance for stationery, communications, audit, banking etc., estimate at KES 750 per month. An audit fee of KES 15,000 is estimated for the twelfth month.

d. General Expenses: Including licenses, permits, insurance, transport, etc., estimated at KES 500 per month. (Note, interest and financing expenses are not included).

e. Repairs and Maintenance: Based on 3 percent of capital equipment, approximately KES 200,000, KES 500 per month.

f. Rent: A nominal charge of KES 1,000 would be charged for rent.

g. Annual Depreciation

		Cost KES	Depr. Rates (Percent)	Depr. KES
1.	Processing Vat	18,000	20	3,600
2.	Milk Cans	22,000	10	2,200
3.	Sealing Equipment	41,000	20	8,200
4.	Lifting Equipment	5,000	10	500
5.	Fridge	15,000	20	3,000
6.	Quality Contr. Equipment	20,000	20	4,000
7.	Weighing Scale	7,000	20	1,400
8.	Misc. Equipment	3,400	20	680
9.	Transport Crates	7,200	10	720
10.	Office Equipment	10,000	10	1,000
	Total:	78,320		24,400

Depreciation per month is rounded to KES 2,000 per month.

ASSUMPTIONS TO THE CASHFLOW PROJECTIONS

1. Milk Price: The same milk price assumptions are used for the income and expenditure projection, i.e., based on giving farmers the farm gate prices they currently receive from marketing milk to the KCC through the group. This is shown in the cash flow.

2. Milk Volume: It is assumed that the premises will be ready in July (month 1) but that no milk is brought while staff are training. Purchases are increased slowly as follows.

Month	1	50 liters	Per day
	2	100 liters	Per day
	3	200 liters	Per day
	4	400 liters	Per day
	5	500 liters	Per day
	6	500 liters	Per day

3. Inflows
    a. Equity/Loans: It is assumed that these are available for all capital purchases. Equity and loans inflow include KES 20,000 for working capital.
    b. Sales are as per the income and expenditure projections. It is assumed milk is paid for in the same month it is bought.

4. Outflows
    a. Total variable costs as detailed in the income and expenditure projections based on the milk volume bought as the project starts. See no. 2 above. Payments are made immediately.
    b. Total fixed costs as detailed in the income and expenditure projections excluding depreciation.
    c. Capital expenditure. Expenditure on capital assets in order to establish the project is assumed to be pre-month one.
    d. Loan or overdraft repayments are scheduled as detailed in the projection.
    e. Operating cash flow: This is cash used or generated by the project operations; it does not include capital repayments.

5. Closing Cash: Details cash available to service loans, purchase further capital equipment, provide return on equity contributions, or pay milk delivery bonus.

ENGINEER CHEESE CO	PROJECTED INCOME AND EXPENDITURE AND CASHFLOW											
MONTH	1	2	3	4	5	6	7	8	9	10	11	12
Milk purchase price	2.5	2.5	2.5	2.5	2.6	2.6	2.6	2.7	2.7	2.8	2.8	2.9
Milk Selling price	5.25	5.25	5.25	5.25	5.25	5.25	5.25	5.25	5.25	5.25	5.25	5.25
Milk volume	1500	3000	6000	12000	13000	13000	13000	13000	13000	13000	13000	13000
INCOME	7875	15750	31500	63000	68250	68250	68250	68250	68250	68250	68250	68250
EXPENSES												
Var. Costs-Milk Purch	3750	7500	15000	30000	33800	33800	33800	35100	35100	36400	36400	37700
Wastage	236.25	472.5	945	1890	2047.5	2047.5	2047.5	2047.5	2047.5	2047.5	2047.5	2047.5
Culture	15	30	60	120	130	130	130	130	130	130	130	130
Firewood	150	300	600	1200	1300	1300	1300	1300	1300	1300	1300	1300
Water	0	0	0	0	0	0	0	0	0	0	0	0
Packaging	600	1200	2400	4800	5200	5200	5200	5200	5200	5200	5200	5200
Detergents	30	60	120	240	260	260	260	260	260	260	260	260
Qual cont chem	22.5	45	90	180	195	195	195	195	195	195	195	195
Transport	450	900	1800	3600	3900	3900	3900	3900	3900	3900	3900	3900
Dairy Board Cess	30	60	120	240	260	260	260	260	260	260	260	260
Total Variable Costs	5283.75	10567.5	21135	42270	47092.5	47092.5	47092.5	48392.5	48392.5	49692.5	49692.5	50992.5
Contribution	2591.25	5182.5	10365	20730	21157.5	21157.5	21157.5	19857.5	19857.5	18557.5	18557.5	17257.5
FIXED COSTS												
Sal. -S/Prod. Tech.	1000	1000	1000	1000	1000	1000	1200	1200	1200	1200	1200	1200
Sal -Prod. Tech. (2)	1400	1400	1400	1400	1400	1400	1600	1600	1600	1600	1600	1600
Watchman	500	500	500	500	500	500	600	600	600	600	600	600
Personnel expenses	820	820	820	820	820	820	820	820	820	820	820	820
AUDIT FEES												15000
Office Expenses	750	750	750	750	750	750	750	750	750	750	750	750
General Expenses	625	625	625	625	625	625	625	625	625	625	625	625
Re. & Main	500	500	500	500	500	500	500	500	500	500	500	500

ENGINEER CHEESE CO — PROJECTED INCOME AND EXPENDITURE AND CASHFLOW

MONTH	1	2	3	4	5	6	7	8	9	10	11	12	
Interest on O/D	750	801	837	801	634	460	283	111	8	0	0	0	
Rent	1000	1000	1000	1000	1000	1000	1000	1000	1000	1000	1000	1000	
Depreciation	2000	2000	2000	2000	2000	2000	2000	2000	2000	2000	2000	2000	
Total Fixed Costs	9345	9396	9432	9396	9229	9055	9378	9206	9103	9095	9095	24095	
Surplus	-6753.75	-4213.5	933	11334	11928.5	12102.5	11779.5	10651.5	10754.5	9462.5	9462.5	-6837.5	
CASHFLOW FORECAST													
OPENING CASH	0	0	0	0	0	0	0	0	0	12651	25414	36876	40339
EQUITY	150000												
LOAN	80000												
Milk Sales	7875	15750	31500	63000	68250	68250	68250	68250	68250	68250	68250	68250	
TOTAL INFLOWS	230000	7875	15750	31500	63000	68250	68250	68250	68250	68250	68250	68250	68250
OUTFLOWS													
Capital Expenditure	210000												
Total Var Exp	5284	10568	21135	42270	47093	47093	47093	48393	48393	49693	49693	50993	
Tot Fix Costs less Depr.	7345	7396	7432	7396	7229	7055	7378	7206	7103	7095	7095	22085	
Total Outflows	210000	12629	17964	28567	49666	54322	54148	54471	55599	55496	56788	56788	73078
Cash from Operations	20000	-4754	-2222	2933	13334	11929	14103	13779	12651	12763	11463	11463	-4838
CLOSING CASH	0	0	0	0	0	0	0	0	12651	25414	36877	40339	43501

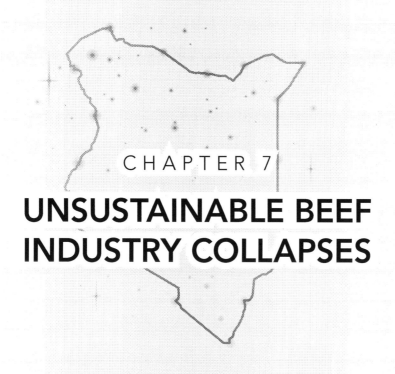

CHAPTER 7

UNSUSTAINABLE BEEF INDUSTRY COLLAPSES

ALLIED RANCHING AND KENYA CATTLE

Allied Ranching was a ranch services company registered in 1975 and owned by among others seven Taita ranches (i.e. Taita, Rukinga, Kasigau, Mgeno, Maungu, Lualenyi, Sagalla), Theta Group, and Technoserve. Each shareholder had made an equal equity contribution to establish Allied Ranching. The objects of the company were to provide services and goods to the seven group ranches and conduct any other business beneficial to ranchers in Taita and the community.

Technoserve was given the mandate to manage Allied Ranching including designing management, accounting, financial control, and record keeping systems for member ranches and providing range management support services to member ranchers. Other Technoserve duties included establishing an engineering center to repair and service vehicles from member ranches and other vehicles in the area.

The business of Allied Ranching was also to include procurement and selling of acaricices[13] and other ranch inputs. Technoserve was to be paid a nominal fee for providing these services. From its inception, Technoserve had provided general managers, financial and range management experts, and extension services to Allied Ranching.

After Technoserve appointed me the general manager of Allied Ranching, I established a radio communication system so all seven ranches would be connected with headquarters. Allied had a staff person manning the radio system center in Voi until ten every night. The service was so important that even the local police department used it to communicate with their personnel in the vicinity of the ranches. This radio communication system was financed by the Agricultural Finance Corporation (AFC). The seven ranches were also beneficiaries of AFC loans under the Group Farms Rehabilitation Project of the World Bank Group.

The Kenyan government established the AFC in 1963 as a statutory body to assist in the development of agriculture by making loans to individual farmers, cooperative societies, and agricultural industry companies. AFC loans were generally secured by land.

One of the large-scale lending programs, the Group Farms Rehabilitation Project, which was initiated in 1975 and partly financed by the World Bank Group, was designed to provide large-scale loans to finance infrastructural development of rangelands to include water supplies, rangelands development including fencing and paddocking, the purchase of young steers for fattening, vehicle and equipment purchases, radio communication systems, and the ranches' operational expenses.

On the marketing side was the Kenya Meat Commission (KMC), which would absorb all beef cattle production in Kenya. The KMC was formed in 1950 through an act of parliament with the objective of providing a ready market for livestock farmers and providing high-quality meat and meat products to consumers locally and overseas. At one time, the KMC exported live cattle to countries such as Saudi Arabia.

The KMC, as a public institution, was by far the oldest and the most experienced meat processor in Kenya and the larger East African region. Its

---

[13] Acaricides are chemicals used to kill ticks on livestock.

headquarters was in Athi River, on the outskirts of Nairobi, with a branch in Mombasa to provide a market for coastal livestock.

In the 1970s, beef production in coastal Kenya, geared to increase, was concentrated in the seven Taita ranches listed above. Other private ranches existed, but these seven were the largest and were owned by groups of the Taita community. On an operational basis, these ranches procured young steers for fattening from some northern ranching areas especially from the Kulalu area. On average, these steers would be fattened over eighteen to twenty-four months and be sold to the KMC or private butchers.

AFC loans were badly designed; loan payments were required from the eighteenth month after the ranchers' drawdown of their credit. Consequently, loan arrears began to build up quickly because of the loan package design and other ranch management problems. Additionally, the KMC got into financial problems rendering it incapable of paying the ranchers on time. Private butchers sprang up and started exploiting the ranchers who had no other outlet for their fattened steers. What could be done to save these ranchers?

Within a few years, it became obvious that the AFC loans could not be serviced as required by the group's ranches. Additionally, these loans were given without an adequate moratorium period. Ranch loans in other countries are normally disbursed with a reasonable moratorium period of between ten and twenty years while AFC loan repayments were supposed to start within the first cycle of eighteen to twenty-four months; there was no way these ranches could make loan repayments according to AFC terms. As Allied Ranching's general manager, I sought ways to have AFC refinance these ranches and establish a moratorium under the refinanced programs. AFC was adamant about this proposal citing its obligations to the government of Kenya concerning this World Bank credit.

Technoserve identified a British source of funding, Commonwealth Development Corporation (CDC), which was willing to provide funding under very favorable terms to the ranches. CDC assigned a project officer to work with a team from Technoserve to develop a proposal to fund rehabilitation and development of the ranch industry in coastal Kenya.

This proposal called for these measures.

- Establishment of Kenya Cattle Limited, an outfit to manage all the seven ranches as a single unit. Each ranch would have to consent to this arrangement before any disbursement of funds. Rainfall statistics from 1900 on indicated that the rainfall pattern over the seven ranches was not uniform; some parts of the ranches got rain at certain periods of the year while others remained dry. Managing the entire seven-ranch area as a single unit would provide the opportunity to manage grazing in accordance with the rainfall distribution in the area.
- Paying off all outstanding AFC loans and injecting new money to finance activities in the new Kenya Cattle business plan.
- Granting Kenya Cattle a moratorium of between fifteen and twenty years. This would enable Kenya Cattle an opportunity to accumulate cash reserves to start paying off the loan comfortably.
- Kenya Cattle would be managed by professional ranch management initially provided by Technoserve through a management agreement. A board of directors would oversee the management of Kenya Cattle and require Technoserve to provide only mutually acceptable staffing to Kenya Cattle.

Meetings were held with AFC senior management in Nairobi, and it was determined that the idea of Kenya Cattle as the future of livestock development efforts in coastal Kenya seemed to be the way to go. Meetings were also held with the member ranches, and all seemed ready to go with this new idea on ranch development in coastal Kenya. However, local politics started scuttling the idea of Kenya Cattle. Among their allegations were these.

- The chair of the Allied Ranching board, a local person, was using Kenya Cattle as a springboard to getting political mileage and depose a sitting member of parliament.

- Though AFC headquarters supported this new strategy of repaying the ranches' loan obligations, AFC on the ground felt they were losing control of the ranches and quietly mobilized members to fight the project.
- Individual ranch companies said that the new Kenya Cattle would make them lose their identity and eventually lose ownership of their group ranch.

Amid these selfish motives, a general meeting called to approve Kenya Cattle as the new approach to ranch development in Taita District rejected the project. That relegated the livestock industry to doom as the Taita ranches were soon choked out by the amassed AFC loan arrears, and it eventually died.

CHAPTER 8

HOW A WELL-MANAGED TURKANA FISHERMEN COOPERATIVE PAID DIVIDENDS TO MEMBERS IN 1980–1981

Anthropology sources say that Turkana is the cradle of humankind based on fossils collected from the area. Lake Turkana is three hundred kilometers long and fifty kilometers wide. Its depth of 358 feet makes it the deepest lake in Kenya. It is the largest lake in Kenya though Lake Victoria, which Kenya shares with Tanzania and Uganda, is larger. It is also the world's largest desert lake. Its water is potable but not very palatable.

The Turkana Fishermen's Cooperative Society (TFCS) was formed in the 1970s to develop and market fish from the lake and uplift the welfare of the Turkana people. However, cold-storage facilities were essential if the fish were to reach market in good condition. However, sun-dried Nile perch, produced to meet the shortfall in fish demand among the Luo community around Lake Victoria, does not require refrigeration.

In the 1970s and early 1980s, the TFCS received colossal amounts of donor funds from NORAD (the Norwegian Agency for Development Cooperation). NORAD is a directorate under the Norwegian Ministry of Foreign Affairs. Its task is to ensure effective foreign aid with quality assurance and evaluation.

The actual amount expended in the form of donor funds to the TFCS excluding technical assistance amounts was over $2,530,000, of which $1,320,000 was spent on establishing the Kalokol ice-making, freezing, and cold-storage plant including a complex of buildings, offices, and workshop.

About 90 percent of the lake's inflow comes from the Omo River, which is entirely in Ethiopia. It enters the lake at its northern end creating a swampy delta. The eastern shores are rugged and rocky with few sheltered bays. The western shore consists of exposed sandy beaches interrupted by the eight-mile Ferguson's Gulf. The seasonal Turkwell and Kerio Rivers enter the lake from its western shores.

There are about twelve fish species commercially caught in Lake Turkana, but tilapia is particularly targeted because of its popularity in the local communities and market destinations in Kenya. Top predators also have tilapia as a key component of their diets. The lake's crocodile population, one of the largest remaining in Africa, was during a census in the late 1960s estimated to consume some 2,000 to 4,000 metric tons of fish annually of which 90 percent were tilapia.

Ferguson's Gulf is designated as a bird sanctuary, where aquatic birds and especially pelicans are considered the most important predators of tilapia (Balarin 1979). Although there are no quantitative impact studies on Lake Turkana, the presence of thousands of pelicans has been reported in the lake (Kolding 1982), and it has been estimated that a pelican can consume about half of a metric ton of tilapia per year (Vareschi 1979). The plentiful Nile perch also prey on tilapia at a rate of 10,000 to 14,000 metric tons per year (Hopson 1982). Given that tilapia occur mainly in the five-meter depth contour of sheltered lagoons around the lake, their contribution to Lake Turkana food system is quite impressive.

Though the Turkana are not traditionally fishermen, they are efficient at it with their artisanal craft and gear and are fast learners. They are able to cross the lake to access fishing grounds off the eastern, northern, and southern shores.

To the extreme north of the lake, beyond Todenyang and at the border between Kenya and Ethiopia, the Merille tribespeople in Ethiopia are the main fishers of the Omo River mouth and delta. The northern shoreline of the lake fluctuates greatly; the lake is almost entirely in Kenya during low lake levels, but at flooding times, a significant part of the lake is in Ethiopia. Merille fishers, therefore, often cross the border to follow the lake since the common understanding is that this northern part of the lake is in Ethiopia, and there are no clear boundary markers. This causes serious conflicts between Turkana and Merille fishers.

The conflict situation is exacerbated by traditional beliefs; a Merille man is considered to be brave and mature and hence ready for marriage if he can prove he has killed a Turkana man. Sporadic attacks on Turkana fishermen in these northern waters have been going on for a long time. Considering that the northern waters are the richest fishing grounds and that most large fish migrate there to spawn, most fish catches come from there. A resolution of the conflict between the Turkana and the Merille would therefore greatly help to improve the livelihood of many Lake Turkana fishers.

On the northeastern shores of the lake, the Dassanach tribe forms the main fishers' community. The main fishing point in this region is around Illaret. The Gabra tribe lives to the east of the Sibiloi National Park, which extends to the eastern part of Lake Turkana as a marine reserve. The Gabra are not traditional fishers, and fishing around Koobi Fora, Allia Bay, and Moite is mainly undertaken by Turkana fishers, who easily sail there from Kalokol owing to its proximity. The regions around Allia Bay and Moite also act as the main fish-drying areas for Turkana fishers. There have been several reported incidents of attacks on fishermen by surrounding tribes such as the Gabra and the Boran. Since these communities are not fishermen traditionally, these attacks were not usually over fishing grounds but rather for the theft of food rations in the expedition boats or from temporary camps set up at the shores by fishermen drying their catch.

Despite these odds, the TFCS is able to get sufficient quantities of fish from the following centers along the lake: Kalokol, Kataboi, Namadak, Lowarengak, and Tordenyang. Ferguson's Gulf, the home of the tilapia, was until early 1980 supplying most of the tilapia catch in the area.

TURKANA FISHERMEN'S COOPERATIVE SOCIETY LIMITED

"Teach a Kenyan cattle herder [the Turkana] how to fish and you'll feed him for life."[14] That was at least what NORAD believed in the 1980s, when it built a fish-processing factory on the shores of Lake Turkana in northwestern Kenya.

> In an attempt to develop one of East Africa's poorest regions, the Norwegian government saw a golden opportunity in the huge but virtually unused lake teeming with fish. It built a fish-freezing and processing plant and set about teaching Turkana's largely pastoral communities how to exploit the lake's fish stocks to bring hard cash into the poverty-stricken region.

> "Norway felt this is a district that has been neglected by the state," Pippi Soegaard, first secretary of the NORAD in Kenya, told Reuters on a trip to Turkana.

It was under these conditions that NORAD requested Technoserve to provide management services to the TFCS. At the time of our appointment, Ferguson's Gulf was the major part of the lake producing big tilapia catches. Other types of fish caught at Lake Turkana included Nile perch. The fishing collection centers were Kalokol, Namadak, Kataboi, Lowarengak, and Tordoenyang. Let us however look at fishing in Lake Turkana as the backdrop of our intervention in the TFCS.

NORAD AND TFCS

NORAD built a fish-processing factory in Kalokol, the main collection center for tilapia and the hub of fish catches on the eastern side of the lake. The factory had ice-making capabilities to preserve the fish for transport to markets in Nairobi and other major centers in Kenya.

Fish products included fresh fish, salted fish (mainly for the export market in the Congo), and sun-dried fish for the Nyanza Province populations. Fresh

---

[14] This comes from https://www.redorbit.com/news/science/456246/kenyas_turkana_learns_from_failed_fish_project/....**Foot.

fish was transported from as far north as Tordenyang while sun-dried fish came from centers such as Namadak, Kataboi, Lowarengak, and others on the eastern side of the lake such as Allia Bay and Moite.

Upon my appointment to the TFCS management team, I faced some major tasks.

- Designing and implementing management, accounting, record keeping, and financial control systems and training staff on the systems.
- Writing and updating accounting and management reports.
- Designing a system for recording members' transactions and ensuring prompt payments to the fishermen.
- Evaluating fish production systems both from fishing and at the factory.
- Reviewing marketing systems for fresh, salted, and sun-dried fish. There were instances of wrong records of fresh and salted fish leaving the factory causing great losses to the cooperative and hence the fishermen. Equally, sun-dried fish traders buying from the society's stores had on many occasions benefitted from faulty weighing machines causing more losses for the cooperative and hence the fishermen.

Within three months of the management team's assignment, the first accounts in years were produced including a trial balance without suspense accounts, an income and expenditure statement, and a balance sheet. An audit was also carried out within nine months of our appointment. Within a year, we received authority from the Commissioner for Cooperative Development to pay a dividend in excess of 10 percent. We recommended that TFCS fishermen buy glass-bottomed boats and stronger, better fishing gear for greater fish production.

At that point, the Technoserve team was withdrawn. Unfortunately, the fishermen, with that dividend money in their pockets, abandoned fishing and retreated to their traditional nomadic lifestyles to raise camels, cattle, goats and sheep. Coupled with this was the drying of the Ferguson's Gulf wiping out the tilapia from their breeding grounds.

The collapse of the TFCS also confirmed:

Despite living near one of Africa's biggest lakes, the Turkana people traditionally do not fish. Like other Nilotic peoples in the Horn of Africa, they are semi-nomadic pastoralists who live off the milk, blood and meat of their herds. Even today, few Turkana fish commercially. Moreover, this confirmed what young Philip Ayane (22), (who lives in the remote village of Nandapal) and said "If you fish it means you are poor because you have no livestock,". "Mostly, it is people who have lost everything to drought who go fishing, when there's no other choice."[15]

---

[15] https://www.redorbit.com/news/science/456246/kenyas_turkana_learns_from_failed_fish_project/....

CHAPTER 9

SOUND MANAGEMENT SYSTEMS FOR SAVINGS AND CREDIT SOCIETIES

HARAMBEE COOPERATIVE SAVINGS AND CREDIT COOPERATIVE SOCIETY (HCSCC)

In 1978, I was hired by Technoserve as a project advisor. My first assignment was to work as a member of a Technoserve management team charged with designing and implementing management, accounting, and financial control systems for Harambee Cooperative Savings and Credit Cooperative Society (HCSCC). In 1978, it was placed under a management commission by the commissioner for cooperative development because of general and financial mismanagement by the society's elected officials. Let us look at some background of the parties concerned in the community-owned and sustainability concepts.

At that time, the Commissioner for Cooperative Development (CCD) was a Kenyan government official appointed by the minister for cooperative development under the Cooperative Societies Act. His powers were defined in that act and by the Cooperative Societies Rules of 1969 that stipulated the operational procedures for all cooperatives. The law gave the CCD overbearing powers in the registration and management of cooperatives.

Besides having the power to register, amalgamate, and deregister cooperatives, the commissioner had to approve annual budgets of the cooperatives, authorize borrowing and expenditures, audit the company's accounts, monitor their financial performance, and even replace elected cooperative societies' officials with management commissions at his or her pleasure. In the case of HCSCC, the CCD had invoked his power to remove elected officials and replace them with an appointed management commission.

SAVINGS AND CREDIT COOPERATIVES

At that time, a group of people with a common bond (meaning in this case a common employer) could apply to the commissioner for cooperative development and be registered as a savings and credit society under Kenyan law. As long as a group could demonstrate a common bond and a willingness of the employer to remit salary deductions to an entity, the commissioner would readily register that organization as a savings and credit cooperative. The registered society would also be required to adopt model governing bylaws.

HCSCC, formed in 1970, drew its membership from employees of the Office of the President and other government ministries using the centralized Kenyan government payroll system. Over the years, the society fell into general and financial mismanagement problems leading to the replacement of its elected officials by a management commission appointed by the commissioner of cooperative development. Let us look at the law in relation to the powers of the commissioner of cooperative development.

POWERS OF THE COMMISSIONER FOR
COOPERATIVE DEVELOPMENT

The Cooperative Societies Act of 1966 and the Cooperative Rules of 1969 outlined the administrative parameters and sanctions for cooperatives. The act covers a wide range of issues. It sets out procedures to be followed when registering a cooperative and powers of the commissioner of cooperatives to accept, reject, or cancel registration.

The commissioner can require any primary society to form or join a cooperative union. He must approve any amendment in the bylaws of a cooperative. Members' rights and liabilities and the duties of registered societies are laid out in detail. No member is allowed to hold more than a fifth of the share capital of a society, and each member is allowed one vote regardless of the number of shares he holds.

The commissioner approves or appoints the auditors of all registered societies. The act also details procedures for amalgamation, division and distribution of societies, measures to be followed in lending and banking cooperative funds, conditions for levying charges, the settlement of disputes, and the avenues open to cooperatives for appeal to the minister of cooperatives. After an inquiry under Section 61 of the act, the commissioner can remove the committee from office and replace it with a management commission to run the society.

The Cooperative Societies Rules of 1969 further specify the powers of the commissioner and the conduct of cooperative affairs in terms of how they should conduct their general meetings, constitute their committees, and use cooperative property and funds. Societies are required to submit monthly trial balances and annual returns to the commissioner. The latter or a person nominated by him must authorize expenses over KES 100 for primary societies and KES 500 for cooperative unions. The commissioner has the right to fix terms and conditions of service for all graded employees in the movement as well as the right to approve loans and conditions under which loans may be obtained from nonmembers.

Under section 61 of the act, some of the general and financial management problems included the following.

- irregularities in election of officials
- favoritism in hiring personnel (many employees were unqualified and in many cases close relatives of elected officials; nepotism seemed the order of the day)
- irregularities in loan granting characterized by favoritism in granting loans and complete disregard of any loan policy

- loans favoring senior officials who used their positions to influence society officials who were their subordinates
- refinancing of loans and increasing default rates
- loan backlogs due to poor cash flows
- poor cash flow triggered by a high loan default rate caused by loan deductions not initiated and/or removed from the government computer payroll system

Consequently, the commissioner invoked the powers conferred to him by the Cooperative Societies Act by removing all elected committee members and appointing a management commission to run the affairs of the HCSCC. Some of the appointed members of the management commission were permanent secretaries and senior government officials from government ministries. These very busy high-ranking government personnel decided to contract Technoserve under a management agreement to do the following.

- rehabilitate and design management, accounting, and financial control systems
- manage and implement the designed systems
- hire and train personnel on the systems and eventually run the savings and credit cooperative
- provide monitoring services after completion of the management contract

The strategies adopted by the management team included the following.

- The design of model bylaws for HCSCC. The design included the following items.
  - duties and responsibilities of members
  - elections of an HCSCC central management committee and defining their duties and responsibilities; the various subcommittees including a credit committee, an education committee, and a supervisory committee, and other subcommittees as may be elected from the central management committee
- The role of the management committee in reference to the
  - management of HCSCC

- o   annual general meetings and powers of members
- o   accounts of the HCSCC
- o   employees of the HCSCC
- The design of a loans policy with roles of the central management committee, the credit committee, the supervisory committee, and staff of HCSCC
- Loan policy to include types of loans and eligibility and defining what were emergency loans, school fees loans, and development loans. It was necessary to define each of the types of loans and eligibility among applicants.
- Loan processing including required guarantees
- Design and implementation of management, accounting, and financial control systems
- Institution of a loan reinstatement and recovery system. One of the causes of the HCSCC's collapse was the high loan default rate, which was in the region of 75 percent. Many loans given to members had not been put into the computer for deductions or were removed from the computer resulting in a high loan default rate. Working with the government of Kenya's payroll staff, we put a system in place to provide monthly computer printouts with schedules of individual outstanding loans, shares contributions and balances, interest recoveries, and a special by-product showing loans input in the computer each month and loans removed from the government payroll system.
- Hire and train staff in the implementation of the installed management, accounting, and financial control systems

Above all, we trained the central management committee (the management commission, whose membership included the top civil servants) to seek loans from banks rather than from HCSCC and allow only the lower-paid members to get loans from the society. In the period prior to our management team taking over the operations of HCSCC, senior civil servants imposed themselves on elected officials who were their subordinates and got loans without regard to any loans policy but because of their positions.

With the implementation of these systems and training of the management commission, the HCSCC was able to get back on its feet and regularly approve and disburse loans to members weekly, reinstate defaulted loans, and reduce the default rate to less than 15 percent of outstanding loans. It became clear that cooperatives should be managed like businesses with timely management and accounting reports.

I would like to share with you an article published by one of the Nation Media Group of Kenya's newspapers. This article is a case of mismanagement of Harambee CSCS Limited. The recommendations in the article are just the same as we recommended in the years of which I am speaking.

Civil Servants to Lose Billions in Harambee Sacco Scandal

Kenya's second largest savings and credit society, Harambee SACCO, has been hit by a serious liquidity crisis, putting at risk the more than Sh4 billion belonging to 100,000 government employees. A confidential inspection report compiled by the SACCO Societies Regulatory Authority (SASRA) shows that the SACCO has been using creative accounting tactics to cover up fraud and nonpayment of loans by some members.

The inspection conducted by the regulator between August 27 and September 6 found that the SACCO did not meet nearly all of the prudence parameters and had negative core capital. It also found that Harambee had understated its bad debts, leading to inadequate loan loss provision. The bad debts are attributed to loans that were disbursed without adequate collateral even as members who have waited for loans in vain call for a refund of their deposits.

"The SACCO requires a total loan loss provision of Sh4.13 billion in order to adequately reflect the possible losses from nonperforming loans even before considering the deposits available as collateral," reads the report.

The regulator adds that insiders were skimming cash through automated teller machine transactions and M-Pesa withdrawals. In June this year, the report says the board of directors resolved to borrow Sh1.2 billion from Co-operative Bank, part of which was used to pay dividends of Sh633 million for last year.

The SACCO's Harambee Plaza building, which the Parliamentary Service Commission plans to buy for the expanded National Assembly, was charged to secure the loan.

"These are pointers to the fact that the SACCO is facing acute liquidity problems and possible financial distress, which may impair its stability and existence in the long term, unless quickly and effectively addressed," says the SASRA's inspection report.

Shot Dead

The report implicates Harambee SACCO's chief executive officer, the head of information technology, the finance manager and chief accountant in the mismanagement scam, but does not identify them by name. It recommends a thorough investigation, full reconciliation of the SACCO's transactions and the recovery of billions of shillings belonging to members.

Last week, Harambee SACCO's finance manager, who was due to appear before the Agriculture, Co-operatives parliamentary committee for questioning over the alleged financial scams was shot dead by unknown people days before he made his presentation to the investigating committee.

SASRA found that Harambee SACCO operated without an internal audit function and the current internal auditor is not registered with the Institute of Certified Public Accountants of Kenya.

The internal auditor was also the SACCO's principal front office services activities (Fosa) manager until June this year, creating a conflict of interest because he was expected to audit a department that he was supervising. The inspectors believe the management deliberately falsified or expunged crucial records with the intention of concealing the true financial condition of the Sacco. As at the time of the inspection, Harambee SACCO had a total loan portfolio of Sh9.81 billion, out of which 29.5 percent or Sh2.89 billion was considered lost because the loans had not been paid for more than 360 days. The inspection, however, found that only 14 percent or Sh1.37 billion of the loan portfolio was performing. Under SASRA prudence guidelines, the level of non-performing debts should not be more than 5 percent. The inspection further found that the SACCO's management information system (MIS) had not been properly configured to produce accurate loan classification reports.

"This has the effect of leading to material misrepresentation of the overall financial position of the SACCO at any given time," the report adds. SASRA has recommended the discontinuation of three popular loan products—Personal Loan 60, Mkombozi Loan and Jisaidie Loan which have a combined outstanding balance of Sh5.2 billion out of which 92 percent or Sh4.8 billion is not performing. The regulator wants the three products stopped by the end of this month and the lending procedures reviewed before they are reintroduced with the approval of the authority.

The report shows that loans borrowed by members of the Ministry of Youth were the most prone to delinquency (81 percent) followed by those disbursed to members of the Immigration department (71 percent), Kenya Police employees (63 percent), Office of the President (59 percent) and Kenya Defense Forces (57 percent). The SACCO draws its membership mainly from government employees including those working in the Office of the President, Department of Defense and National Police Service which includes the Administration and Kenya Police.

"Majority of these members are salary-based public servants and there ought to be minimal incidence of loan default if any," adds the SASRA inspection report. Harambee SACCO employees had at the time of inspection borrowed Sh232.5 million, more than a third (Sh84 million) of which was nonperforming. The report blames the management for not disclosing the extent of the loan default to the board of directors whose members are also thought to be compromised by overdrafts in their Fosa Accounts. At the time of inspection 1,607 Fosa accounts were overdrawn to the tune of Sh20 million. At least Sh6.3 million of the amounts had benefited staff members and Sh593, 000 related to five members of the board of directors.

"The overdrawing of accounts by directors and senior members of staff is irregular and amounts to granting credit facilities without following due process which is tantamount to abuse of office," notes the SASRA report.

Poor management practices have led to discontentment among members with 954 members with savings of Sh127 million having applied for refunds and to leave the Sacco. There was also a loan backlog of Sh29.3 million, excluding loans that were awaiting disbursement.[16]

ARDHI COOPERATIVE SAVINGS AND CREDIT SOCIETY (ACSCS)

Because of the success of HCSCC, the elected management committee of Ardhi Cooperative Savings and Credit Society (ACSCS) requested Technoserve to provide management services to Ardhi. At the time, ACSCS drew its membership from employees of the Ministry of Lands and Settlement and its elected officials from middle management of that ministry. Because of their positions at the ministry, they were conditioned to grant loans to senior officials in the ministry and to other members recommended for loans by these senior personnel.

---

[16] "Civil Servants to Lose Billions in Harambee SACCO Scandal," *Business Daily Africa*, November 4, 2012.

The Ministry of Cooperative Development officials were not giving these elected officials the support they needed to counter pressure from their bosses. This loan-granting practice created high default rates on the disbursed loans and ill feelings among eligible loan applicants, and it contributed generally to mismanagement of the ACSCS.

The elected officials had learned of the great success of HCSCC through Technoserve management systems and implementation of a loans policy that treated all equally. They also looked up to Technoserve as an independent organization that would provide a buffer against pressures from senior management of the Ministry of Lands and Settlement.

Under the agreement between Technoserve and the ACSCS management committee, I was appointed to head a team of qualified staff to provide the required services. At the time, ACSCS did not have an office of its own. My first assignment was to have a prefabricated office building built on a plot allocated to ACSCS by the Department of Survey of the Ministry of Lands and Settlement.

KENYA UNION OF SAVINGS AND CREDIT COOPERATIVES (KUSCCO)

In 1982, the commissioner for cooperative development invoked his powers as spelled out in the Cooperative Societies Act of 1966 and the Cooperative Societies Rules of 1969 to remove elected members of the management committee of the Kenya Union of Savings and Credit Cooperatives (KUSCCO) and replace them with a management commission.

The fact that the commissioner was appointed by the minister, who was appointed by the president, ensured that the state controlled all the affairs of the cooperative societies. State control was enhanced by international donors to the cooperative movement who preferred to work through the government. To support the management commission, the CCD appointed Technoserve.

KUSCCO CORPORATE INFORMATION

The KUSCCO was registered under the Cooperative Societies Act in 1973 and established as an umbrella organization for all SACCOs (savings and credit cooperatives) in Kenya. The union has since remained the principal national organization recognized as an institution responsible for representing and speaking on behalf of Kenyan SACCOs.

At the time (1982) of the appointment of a management commission, the KUSCCO provided the following services.

- advocacy and representation
- risk management
- bookkeeping services to small-and medium-sized savings and credit cooperatives
- training and education

ADVOCACY AND REPRESENTATION

The KUSCCO at the time had lost a lot of credibility among members, and some even stopped paying their membership dues as the organization could not demonstrate its capability to fulfill its role. Membership dues from savings and credit had therefore declined substantially.

RISK-MANAGEMENT PROGRAM

The KUSCCO had a risk-management program underwritten by the African Confederation of Cooperative Savings and Credit Associations. This organization provided insurance to cover members' savings and loans. The program would pay twice the value of deceased members' shares to their families and clear their outstanding loans. The KUSCCO collected premiums from members, invested the funds, and paid off claims. This program had also failed, which necessitated the birth of another organization, Cooperative Insurance Services, which started competing for the risk-management role of the KUSCCO.

BOOKKEEPING SERVICES

The KUSCCO had branches in Nairobi, Nakuru, Kisumu, Kakamega, and Mombasa that were providing bookkeeping services to affiliated societies at highly subsidized fees. These services were also not satisfactory as there was a backlog of uncompleted accounts and audits such that members sought similar services from other sources even if the fees were higher than KUSCCO's.

TRAINING AND EDUCATION

The KUSCCO had a training program at the Cooperative College of Kenya for committee members and ordinary members supported by a donor, the Konrad Adenauer Foundation, which provided the KUSCCO with funds to host weekend seminars for committee members and training for staff at the Cooperative College of Kenya. This program ran well until abuses started creeping in. The weekend seminars became opportunities for certain people to siphon off money. Many society officials looked at the KUSCCO as the place to go partying during the weekend seminars, which were held at expensive hotels.

APPOINTMENT OF KUSCCO MANAGEMENT COMMISSION

At the time of the appointment of the management commission, the KUSCCO had lost credibility among its members. Many of the members had stopped paying dues and discontinued the risk-management program, and others had withdrawn from KUSCCO's bookkeeping services. Some members were even advocating for the dissolution of the KUSCCO. Revenues to run any activities had therefore dropped significantly.

I was appointed to head the management team at the KUSCCO. The strategies we adopted were as follows.

- design, install, and implement management, accounting, and financial control systems
- hire and train staff on the installed systems

- address the bookkeeping backlogs and update all overdue accounts at the bookkeeping centers around the country
- design a system to keep track of the status of bookkeeping at the centers
- reconcile members' accounts at the bookkeeping centers
- reconcile the risk-management account, identify premium arrears from savings and credit societies and install a system to collect these premiums, reconcile claims payment records, and design a system of prompt claims processing and payment
- review the education program and work with the Konrad Adenauer Foundation on yearly plans and budgets for relevant types of training, which entailed incorporating trainers from the business community to supplement training facilitators from the KUSCCO and the Ministry of Cooperative Development
- design a standardized management, accounting, and financial control policy manual for all savings and credit societies
- have the Ministry of Cooperatives adopt this as the policy to be implemented in all societies in Kenya

Within two years, the KUSCCO was turned around.

- Members resumed paying dues.
- Accounts at the bookkeeping centers were updated with the improved bookkeeping services.
- A management and accounting manual for all savings and credit societies was completed and approved by the ministry for use by all savings and credit societies.
- A streamlined education plan was in place.
- The risk-management program was running to the satisfaction of members.
- A new general manager and other key staff were recruited and trained on the systems as we handed over KUSCCO's management in December 1984.

CHAPTER 10

COFFEE IN KENYA: SUSTAINABILITY—THE COOPERATIVE MANAGEMENT IMPROVEMENT PROJECT

In 1986, the Ministry of Cooperative Development commissioned Technoserve Kenya to carry out a study of the management systems in coffee-marketing cooperative societies in Kenya and make recommendations for better management systems to increase the payout to farmers. This effort, called the Cooperative Management Improvement Project (CMIP), was funded as part of the World Bank Small Coffee Improvement Project (SCIP).

The CMIP fell under the SCIP component designed to strengthen the Ministry of Cooperative Development (MCD) through provision of office equipment, vehicles, and staff necessary to expand and strengthen the Department of Cooperative Development (DCD). The main activities to be strengthened were those that the MCD was responsible for: education, accounting, credit and savings, planning, and management.

One of the best incentives to raise farmers' interest would be to maximize payouts to them. At the time of this project, in 1986, this payout level averaged 75 percent of the auction price of their coffee with considerable variations from as low as 30 percent to as high as 85 percent. However, the expected fall in coffee prices linked with the existing overhead cost to unions and societies would result in a decreased payout to farmers equal to about 60 percent of auction prices.

The MCD had the responsibility of improving the operational activities of unions and societies, and it was in this area that the greatest contribution from the MCD could be made. A direct reduction in overhead costs in the union and societies and the coffee factories would result in a direct increase in payout to farmers. The proposed improvements in the MCD's supervisory capabilities aimed to maintain the payout level at approximately 75 percent of auction prices.

COFFEE GROWING AND MARKETING IN KENYA

Coffee growing was introduced in Kenya around 1900 and has gone through various ups and downs. The industry initially developed along estate lines.[17] By 1935, about 42,000 hectares were planted with Arabica coffee producing approximately 22,000 tons of washed coffee. From 1935 to 1950, the hectarage under coffee declined steadily to 24,000 hectares mainly the result of poor prices.

The sharp rise in prices from 1950 on was responsible for the third phase in coffee development in Kenya. By 1955, production overtook the 1935 level and reached 23,000 tons. During this third phase, the first major diversification of coffee production to smallholders occurred. However, the process was slow. It was not until 1960 that production became really significant in regard to quantity and quality.

By 1964, mature smallholding hectares surpassed the estate hectares, and smallholding production overtook estate production in 1965–66. By 1980, production from the smallholder sector was about the same as the production from the estate sector though the average yields of the smallholder sector were well below those of the estate sector.

In Kenya, coffee is the single most important agricultural commodity in

---

[17] Large coffee estates produced coffee on big tractsof land. Small holder coffee production was undertaken by individuals who owned small land holdings.

terms of its contribution to the gross market value of agricultural produce and in earning foreign exchange. The share of coffee in total annual export earnings has consistently been more than 14 percent since 1972. In 1976, the share increased to 27.8 percent and in 1977 to a record 42.6 percent.

Coffee is also important in terms of employment. Out of about 900,000 people in regular wage employment in the monetary sector in Kenya during 1977, approximately 87,000 were permanent workers in the various parts of the coffee industry. An additional unknown number of workers are involved in casual employment particularly during the picking season.

KENYAN COFFEE MARKETS AND PRICES

The marketing structure is centralized through the Coffee Board of Kenya (CBK), which controls the planting of coffee through a licensing system, takes delivery of all coffee produced, and sells it for export by auction. Its main intermediate agent is the Kenya Planters Cooperative Union (KPCU), which receives parchment coffee[18] from the estates and from smallholders through the local cooperative societies for hulling, grading, and cleaning. All final processing and grading take place in Nairobi, where facilities exist for storage throughout the year. Auctions are normally held every week. The year 1975–76 represented a dramatic year with price records being set and then broken almost weekly. In 1977, prices rose even higher because of the quality of Kenyan coffee, which was reflected in the high prices it commanded in export markets. During the 1970s, there had been a decrease in the coffee-growing areas though it had remained static at around the 86,800 hectares recorded in 1977. The decline was attributed to the following.

- management problems associated with the transfer of production from estates to smallholders
- a coincidental rise in the incidence of coffee berry disease, seriously reducing yields and earnings
- restrictions on new plantings under the International Coffee Agreement, which ended in 1973.

---

[18] Parchment coffee isdried coffee that has not been hulled.

In 1977, the relative areas grown by estates and smallholders were 27,800 (32 percent) and 59,000 (68 percent) hectares. Approximately 270,000 farmers were registered as coffee growers in the 1980s. The remaining registered coffee estates (731 in 1977) have each an average productive area of 40 hectares.

The decline in production 1973–1975 could be attributed specifically to the following.

- poor rainfall (many coffee growing areas suffered drought in 1973)
- escalation in input costs leading to low fertilizer and spray applications and consequential yield reduction and disease recurrence
- increasing problems with labor and handling
- comparatively better prices and payment systems for alternative crops

The greatest potential for increasing output from existing bushes was in the smallholder coffee sector, where average yields were well below potential. Average yields of washed coffee on smallholdings had reached less than 50 percent of that achieved by estates. Productivity in smallholdings was 760 kilograms per hectare on average compared with 1,790 kilograms per hectare on average on estates in 1977. However, production in the smallholder industry did produce mean average yields of up to 1,450 kilograms per hectare per year. The low average productivity was attributed to the 23,000 hectares of neglected coffee holdings.

The KPCU and the Cooperative Production Credit Scheme (CPCS) provided only creditworthy coffee farmers with agricultural supplies on credit. The criteria for these loans were directly linked with past production; neglected holdings therefore did not qualify for access to sufficient input supplies because of former low production levels. A major aim of the government was therefore to reduce this imbalance and raise the coffee earnings of smallholders with neglected holdings. To achieve these aims, it was necessary to analyze the reasons for the poor performance of farmers who owned the neglected holdings.

One main reason appeared to be farmers' dissatisfaction with the services supplied by coffee factories, societies, and unions. Poor management of societies had frequently resulted in low payment rates for coffee delivered because of high overhead costs. In addition, the capacity of the machinery in coffee factories was often not capable of handling the crop, which resulted in either lower quality of coffee produced or farmers being turned away when trying to sell their coffee crop.

The same results were also noticed when factory management was poor. In both cases, the result was a lower payout rate for coffee delivered by smallholder coffee farmers. In the end, the farmer often decided to neglect his coffee and spend more time on other crops.

Coffee growers' cooperative societies were well established throughout the country, but the inefficient management of a number of societies had resulted in a lower payout to the small farmers, thus diminishing the incentive for them to improve production. The sector also had problems of deteriorating quality in previous years because of undercapacity and poor management of the cooperatively owned processing factories.

There existed a wide range in the efficiency of committees and staff of the societies. Individual growers were often inclined to associate themselves only with the most efficient societies. This trend could be halted only by ensuring the administrative efficiency of cooperative organizations and by improving the facilities and capacity of the cooperative factories. That sparked the commissioning of Technoserve to conduct the CMIP.

I was a key member of the teams that traveled to conduct interviews and collect data in the greater Kisii, Bungoma, Baringo, Machakos, Embu, Meru, and Kilifi Districts. Baringo and Kilifi are not coffee-growing districts, but they were included in the study because they would benefit from the management, accounting, financial control, and record-keeping systems and procedures of the coffee industry to be recommended after the study.

Our findings confirmed the existence of poor management, accounting, record-keeping, and financial control systems in practice in all areas we visited. The percentage of farmer payout compared to the prices realized at coffee auctions was extremely low, in some cases as low as 30 percent. The SCIP program in many areas was attractive to management committees of the coffee societies because the prospect of increasing the capacity of a factory (more processing discs[19]) provided them opportunities to make money on the side. While SCIP

---

[19] Most coffee factories were built with a single disc, which removes the covering of coffee beans. Therefore, to increase the capacity of a factory, more discs are required. Usually, vendors inflate the prices of discs to pay bribes to management committee members.

coffee factory loans required an exhaustive analysis of production capacities at the farmer level and production capacities of coffee-processing plants, this was overlooked in many cases as the prospect of making extra money on the side appeared more attractive to the committees and government extension officers. We found cases where coffee societies increased their processing capacities from one disc to three without a corresponding increase in coffee production from members. Since the increased capacity was financed with SCIP loans, this increased the loan obligations to the lending agency, the Cooperative Bank of Kenya, thus reducing funds available for farmer payouts.

Our recommendations included the design and installation of management, accounting, record-keeping, and financial control systems. Upon installation of these systems, we recommended that staff be trained to operate the systems. Equally important was a rigorous assessment of any increases to processing capacities (new processing discs) for all coffee cooperatives. More extension work designed to increase farmers' coffee outputs was to go hand in hand with increasing coffee production.

CHAPTER 11

HORTICULTURE PRODUCTION AND MARKETING

TAITA HILLS HORTICULTURAL PRODUCTION AND MARKETING PROJECT

Many of us viewed small-scale horticultural farmers in Kenya as hard workers but wondered why they were poor. Examples are among the following: French beans farmers at the Yatta furrow, tomato farmers in Karatina/Kerugoya, snow pea farmers in Kieni and Naro Moru, and small-scale flower farmers in South Kinangop.

The reasons farmers continue getting low prices are related to production and marketing problems. Production problems include lack of technical input (quality seeds, fertilizers, pesticides), farm management skills including planting and transplanting technologies, and weeding, harvest, and postharvest handling technology.

Marketing problems include exploitation either by middlemen who pay peanuts to the farmers compared to what they get from the exporters or by unscrupulous exporters who take farmers' produce, never pay them, and give excuses that an overseas buyer did not pay for poor or damaged produce. In one case, an exporter actually made this ridiculous excuse to farmers, "The undercarriage of the plane carrying your produce opened in midair and your flowers fell out." This is what small-scale farmers are subject to, and they have no recourse.

Let us look at horticultural production and marketing in Taita Hills from 1989 to the 1990s and see how farmers benefitted from better production technologies, better management, and better marketing systems. This vegetable production and marketing enterprise is a very good example of a sustainable community-owned enterprise.

My task in Taita District (where I had earlier served as the general manager of Allied Ranching) was to increase quality horticultural production and develop a marketing program to increase the incomes of the people there.

Vegetable production in the Taita Hills had been introduced and promoted by the British colonial powers in Kenya during World War II as a war effort to provide fresh vegetables for British soldiers fighting in Tanganyika. Demand for horticultural products also picked up with the growth of tourist hotels in coastal Mombasa and Malindi. However, Taita horticultural farmers could not meet this increased demand for horticultural produce and benefit from the new markets in the Mombasa and Malindi tourist industry due to poor production technologies for horticultural production and marketing.

The German Technical Cooperation Agency (Gesellschaft für Technische Zusammenarbeit—GTZ) in Kenya, alongside the Ministry of Agriculture, conducted a study that demonstrated that the horticultural industry had great potential in Taita Hills. Neither the ministry nor the GTZ had the capability to implement the project, so they approached Technoserve to do so.

In 1989, Technoserve Kenya signed a contract with the government of Kenya to implement a horticultural development project in Taita Hills funded by a German development bank, Kreditanstalt für Wiederaufbau. With the signing of this contract, the Taita Hills Horticultural Center (THHC) was established. The goal of the project was to provide a better life for the Taita horticultural farmers through increased quality horticultural production, better marketing, and higher farmer payouts. The philosophy behind the collaboration between the farmers and Technoserve Kenya was the transference not of money but of skills. Providing people with the skills that allow them to manage their resources and provide for their families enhances the chances of success.

The usual impediments to farmers in the developing world were present when we undertook this venture: poverty, lack of proper farming techniques, poor soil, crop disease, low-yielding seeds, and the pervasive middlemen who made it hard for hardworking farmers to profit from their labor.

The intervention strategies focused on the following objectives.

- to increase vegetable yields
- to improve the quality of vegetables bound for the market
- to develop an efficient marketing system
- to establish an enterprise to coordinate the day-to-day operations of the project.

According to *Life Lessons of an Immigrant*[20] (p. 192) by John Makilya),

The THHC membership increased from eight hundred to two thousand during the time of our intervention. Vegetable produce grown and marketed included green beans, tomatoes, zucchini, lettuce, onions, carrots, cabbage, eggplant, and some fruits. These products were collected and brought to the center warehouse, graded for quality and uniform size, and then trucked to the bustling Mombasa produce market. Farmers in the Taita Hills planted locally consumed and marketed vegetables, some of which were transported to the Mombasa tourist markets. These tourist markets were also supplied by up-country horticultural sources. Horticultural farmers from central Kenya utilized empty lorry space of trucks driving back to Mombasa, thus lowering transport costs and competing effectively with farmers' produce from Taita Hills. Moreover, the Taita County Council charged levies on produce from Taita Hills being transported to Mombasa. This, too, made Taita horticultural produce more expensive than produce from Central Kenya.

Prior to Technoserve's intervention, horticultural produce yields were very poor, and horticultural markets offered low prices. Studies were carried out to improve production technologies, including inputs (fertilizers, etc.) and high-quality seeds and fertilizers suitable for soils in the area. Demonstration farms were established so that farmers could be trained on nursery management, transplanting techniques, weeding, pesticide use including, harvesting and

---

[20] https://www.archwaypublishing.com/Bookstore/BookDetail.aspx?Book=7622600.

postharvest techniques including storage during transportation to the market. Extension work on farmers' fields was programed and irrigation from runoff rivers was coordinated so that farmers upstream did not divert all the water at the expense of farmers downstream. The farmers' training facility in Ngerenyi in Taita Hills was reactivated and started regular horticultural training programs geared toward improving horticultural production and marketing. Above all, production planning was established to ensure that farmers planted to produce when there were shortages in the market.

CHAPTER 12

HOW SUSTAINABLE BEEKEEPERS COMMUNITY ENTERPRISE BENEFITS MEMBERS

It has often been said that communities in dry areas of Kenya such as Kitui County have very few enterprises they can start as groups and benefit members, but this is not true; beekeeping offers a wonderful opportunity for these communities to develop sustainable beekeeping enterprises. A group of between twenty and thirty can successfully run a beekeeping enterprise. They would need to be registered with the Ministry of Culture and Social services and register governing bylaws, elect a management board, and employ a manager and accountant to manage the day-to-day activities of the enterprise. Let us first go through the process of making honey.

HOW BEES MAKE HONEY

The author is grateful to the Australian Honey Bee Industry Council and in particular its chief executive officer for allowing the use of the following materials about how bees make honey.[21]).

It has been said that except for man, nowhere in the world is there anything to compare with the incredible efficiency of the industry of the honeybee. Inside the beehive each bee has a special job to do and the whole process runs smoothly.

Bees need two different kinds of food. One is honey made from nectar, the sugary juice that collects in the heart of the flowers. The other comes from the anthers of flowers, which contain numerous small grains called pollen. Just as flowers have different colors, so do their pollen.

Let us go with the honeybee from her flower to the hive and see what happens. Most bees gather only pollen or nectar. As she sucks the nectar from the flower, it is stored in her special honey stomach ready to be transferred to the honey-making bees in the hive. If hungry she opens a valve in the nectar "sac" and a portion of the payload passes through to her own stomach to be converted to energy for her own needs.

The bee is a marvelous flying machine. She can carry a payload of nectar or pollen close to her own weight. Consider that even the most advanced design in aircraft can only take off with a load one-quarter of its own weight and you'll appreciate the miracle that the honeybee can remain airborne with such a load.

When her nectar "sacs" are full, the honeybee returns to the hive. Nectar is delivered to one of the indoor bees and is then passed

---

[21] https://honeybee.org.au/education/wonderful-world-of-honey/how-bees-make-honey/.

mouth-to-mouth from bee to bee until its moisture content is reduced from about 70% to 20%. This changes the nectar into honey. Sometimes the nectar is stored at once in cells in the honeycomb before the mouth-to-mouth working because some evaporation is caused by the 32.5°C temperature inside the hive.

Finally, the honey is placed in storage cells and capped with beeswax in readiness for the arrival of newborn baby bees. Pollen is mixed with nectar to make "bee bread" and is fed to the larvae. A baby bee needs food rich in protein if the bee community is to flourish.

Before returning to the flower again for more pollen, the bee combs, cleans and cares for herself? not because she is vain but so she can work more efficiently. Throughout her life cycle, the bee will work tirelessly collecting pollen, bringing it back to the hive, cleaning herself, then setting out for more pollen.

Forager bees start out from the hive for blossom patches when three weeks old. As they live to be only six or seven weeks old they have much work to do and little time in which to do it.

There will be many other bees working at the same time, and the air will be noisy with their droning. It takes 300 bees about three weeks to gather 450 g of honey. On average, a hive contains 40,000 bees.

The Type of Bees

The Queen Bee

The Queen is the center of the hive: She accompanies every-swarm that you see. The Queen is also the largest bee and her body is specially formed for egg-laying-so that the eggs can be placed a little above the center of the cells in the honeycomb.

Before depositing her eggs, she inspects each cell to be sure it is properly cleaned by the workers. Just think of her effort and industry!

When, for any reason the colony needs a new Queen; extra royal jelly is fed to chosen larvae in the cells. The first young Queen to emerge from the pupa destroys all other developing Queens in the cells, then sets out on her mating flight after five to twelve days. After mating the young Queen has much to do. With her eggs fertile, she must return swiftly to the hive. The old Queen will have left with a swarm beforehand. The new Queen, closely surrounded by worker bees who feed and groom her, can lay up to one egg every minute day and night.

The Drones

Drones are the future fathers of the bee colony (rather a very small number of them will be). Shorter than the Queen, drones are larger than the workers. They have no accomplishments other than being patient. They cannot make wax, have no proboscis for collecting pollen or nectar, and have no pollen pikes on their legs. They are never called on to defend the hive so they have no need for a sting.

Drones rarely feed themselves – instead, they hold out their tongues and a worker bee places food on it. They are truly gentlemen in waiting. They are waiting for the day when a young Queen will fly from the hive. When a new Queen flies from the hive she joins the drones, who are already circling in drone congregation areas. The swiftest drones will catch and mate with the Queen, but their life is short. After mating, they will float back to earth and be dead by the time they reach the ground. They have helped to bring new life to the colony and their work is finished. The remaining drones return to the hive either to be driven out or to die there during the winter or when a shortage of food occurs.

Worker Bees

The main section of the hind pair of legs has special spines for holding pollen or propolis (a kind of gum). The center legs are the bees' main support, but all six legs are variously equipped with brushes, combs and spurs with which to brush pollen from the eyes, clean the antennae, wipe dust from the wings and pack pollen spines. The tongue and mandibles are used to lick and collect pollen grains from the anthers of flowers, with the result that the pollen grains are moistened with honey and stick together. The pollen is then transferred to the hind legs and held firmly until the forager enters the hive, when it is then packed in cells in the honeycomb.

Worker bees have two heavy spoon shaped jaws which work sideways. The jaws are used for collecting pollen and chewing wax. The abdomen has two important organs – the wax glands and the sting. Wax glands are special cells on the underside of the last four segments of the body. Wax is discharged through these special cells in tiny scales, which are then molded and used in comb building, capping and the cells.

Life in the Hive

In her lifetime, the Queen can produce more than one million eggs. At first, after the eggs are hatched, all the larvae are fed on royal jelly – a milky white fluid made by a gland in the nurse bees' head. This rich food helps larvae to grow strongly. After three days, the workers' diet is changed mainly to pollen and nectar, while the Queens continue to be fed on royal jelly.

On the eighth day, the larva spins itself a silken cocoon and during the next week or two makes the great change from pupa to adult. It gnaws its way out of its cocoon and, as it gains strength, joins the workers in their task of foraging or engineering, nursing the young, converting nectar into honey, cleaning the hive and waiting on the Queen. So, the life cycle goes on!

The Language of Bees

Bees cannot talk. Their language is one of vibration. To indicate distance, the scout bee uses an audible code of buzzes, on a 200 cycle per second note with a pulse rate of 35 to the second. The length of time on a wagtail run and the number of pulses of sound in each buzz indicate distance.

Harvesting Honey

As soon as the honeycomb in the hive is filled with honey and capped with beeswax they are ready to be harvested. Beekeepers regularly inspect their hives to see when the honeycomb can be removed. Honeycomb is removed from the hive and taken to a mobile extracting van or central extracting plant called a "honey house". The wax cappings are removed with a steam heated knife or special revolving blade before the honeycomb is placed in the extractor. The honeycomb is then placed in revolving baskets where the spinning movement throws out the honey by centrifugal force.

Little or no damage is done to the delicate honeycomb by this process and when it is returned to the hive, the bees immediately set about removing any left-over honey plus repairing and polishing each cell in readiness for a new load of honey. Honey collected from the extractor is then strained and left to stand until air bubbles rise. Bubbles and any left-over wax particles are skimmed from the surface and the honey is ready for bottling.

It truly is straight from Nature's storehouse! Most apiarists (beekeepers) send their honey in bulk to city and country packing houses. Some have their own bottling equipment and sell the honey to retail and wholesale stores.

How Does a Bee Find Pollen?

Honeybees prefer to work close to their hive. Beekeepers move hives occasionally to give the bees access to a good floral source. Bees tend to work less than 200 meters from the hive, but can range up to more than 1.5 km away if necessary. Scout bees have the task of finding new nectar sources and head out to check all nearby vegetation. If they find nectar, they return to the hive and pass on the exact location with a remarkably intricate dance routine.

The Dance of the Bee

Once pollen, nectar or water is found, the scout bee returns to the hive and dances on the honeycomb to indicate where the source may be found. Many factors indicate to the worker bee the precise position. Wings vibrating swiftly as the scout bee dances in a circle indicates that the find is within 100 meters of the hive. If the source is further away, the dance will be a "wagtail" roughly in a figure eight with a straight center section. The direction in which she runs the center and the speed of her movements tell how far to fly and in which direction.

CHAPTER 13

ARABUKO SOKOKE: MANY DONORS FOR THE SAME CLIENT—DEPENDENCY?

The Arabuko Sokoke Forest Reserve is located on the coast of Kenya, 110 km north of Mombasa and is protected as a National Forest Reserve. Arabuko Sokoke Forest, covering 41,600 ha, is the largest single block of coastal forest remaining in East Africa.

The **Arabuko Sokoke National Park**, situated at the northwestern edge of the Arabuko Sokoke Forest Reserve was gazetted only in the late 1980s and in fact straddles the Forest Reserve boundary, with about 50% lying outside the boundary. This outer section actually lies outside an electric elephant fence installed in 2006/7 and is now fully inhabited by local communities to the extent that there is no sign on the ground to show where the National Park begins or ends. The National Park doesn't add any particular protection to the forest which is the largest fragment of coastal forest (420 square km) left in East Africa.

The Forest Reserve, on the other hand, is jointly managed by the Kenya Forest Service, Kenya Wildlife Service, National Museums of Kenya and the Kenya Forest Research Institute and is one of the better protected forests in Kenya. The forest was first protected as a Crown Forest in 1943, and was gazetted in the 1960s. The forest is threatened by the desire for land by local people as 54 villages, whose inhabitants depend on the forest for their subsistence uses. Several national and international conservation organizations are working with the Kenya Wildlife Service to protect the park.[22]

Various donor organizations work in the area and include the following.

The Arabuko–Sokoke Forest Adjacent Dwellers Association (ASFADA) is the forest's Site Support Group (SSG). The group has 3,563 members and is involved in activities such as butterfly farming, beekeeping, tree planting and ecotourism with help from Nature Kenya and the Community Development Trust Fund.

The ASFADA built and manages the Jamii Villas, where visitors can stay or have a meal.

The Friends of Arabuko-Sokoke Forest, a working group of Nature Kenya, also carries out conservation activities in the forest. The group monitors, documents and reports illegal tree felling and poaching of animals, creates awareness about the value of the forest amongst local and international communities, and supports local farming communities and the conservation work of the Kenya Forest Service and Kenya Wildlife Service.

Nature Kenya in partnership with DOF – the BirdLife Partner in Denmark – secured funding from Denmark for a program titled

---

[22] Wikipedia.

"Integrating Livelihoods and Conservation – People Partner with Nature for Sustainable Living". The program's long-term objective is to reduce forest loss in three forested Important Bird and Biodiversity Areas (IBAs) at the Kenyan coast – Arabuko-Sokoke Forest, Dakatcha Woodland and Taita Hills forests – and contribute to best participatory forest management practices for the benefit of all. It is being implemented through partnerships with various government institutions, the Kilifi and Taita–Taveta county governments and site support groups.

This program is supporting 50 beekeeping groups and 26 butterfly farming groups in Arabuko-Sokoke.

Nature Kenya, through funding from the NABU (the BirdLife partner in Germany) has also continued to support improvement of local capacity through diversification of skills. The NABU funded project aims at contributing to the implementation of the Arabuko-Sokoke Forest Elephant Conservation Action Plan.[23]

BIODIVERSITY IN ARABUKO SOKOKE

The Arabuko Sokoke Forest is an area of high endemism, containing endemic mammals, birds and plants. It contains three forest types, mixed forest, *Brachystegia* and *Cynometra*, each of which protects different communities of plants and animals.

It protects many endemic and near endemic species. The Clarke's weaver is completely endemic to the forest, while the eponymous Sokoke scops owl, Sokoke pipiot, and the Amani sunbird and spotted ground thrushare found only here and in a forest fragment in Tanzania. The park adjoins *Mida Creek*, a mangrove forest that is an important shorebird wintering ground, protecting species such as the Terek sandpiper and the crab plover.

---

[23] https://naturekenya.org/2017/02/06/arabuko-sokoke-the-premier-coastal-forest/........Source.

The endearing golden-rumped elephant shrew, an endemic elephant shrew the size of a rabbit, is the most noticeable of the park's endemic mammals; the Sokoke bushy-tailed mongoose and Aders's duiker (found only here and in Zanzibar) are more elusive. The forest also has savannah elephants, African civets, as well as Sokoke's baboons and vervet monkeys. The park is also recognized as an outstanding center of amphibian diversity.[24]

Economic activities that could be enhanced to benefit the communities in the area include the following.

- butterfly farming, beekeeping, tree planting, and ecotourism with help from Nature Kenya and the Community Development Trust Fund.
- Fifty beekeeping groups and twenty-six butterfly farming groups in Arabuko-Sokoke supported by Integrating Livelihoods and Conservation—People Partner with Nature for Sustainable Living, implemented through partnerships with various government institutions, the Kilifi and Taita–Taveta county governments, and site-support groups.

The Arabuko–Sokoke Forest Adjacent Dwellers Association (ASFADA) is the forest's Site Support Group (SSG) with 3,563 members is involved in activities such as butterfly farming, beekeeping, tree planting and ecotourism with help from Nature Kenya and the Community Development Trust Fund.[25]

There is always a problem with many donors working with the same communities without coordination. A review of all activities in Arabuko Sokoke is necessary to avoid duplication and maximize benefits to the local communities. It is difficult to assess whether communities benefit from all the donors in the area and avoid the cost of assistance becoming higher than the benefits to the community.

---

[24] https://en.wikipedia.org/wiki/Arabuko_Sokoke_National_Park.
[25] https://naturekenya.org/2017/02/06/arabuko-sokoke-the-premier-coastal-forest/.

CHAPTER 14

MORE SUSTAINABILITY: SOCIOECONOMIC IMPACT ASSESSMENT OF THE EL NIÑO EMERGENCY PROJECT

The ENEP was a project designed by the World Bank to support the Kenyan government's ongoing efforts to mitigate the serious effects of flooding attributed to the El Niño phenomenon of 1997/98. The project aimed to minimize life-threatening conditions in twenty-three impacted districts of Kenya and the province of Nairobi by restoring as much of the previously existing potable water supply as possible and to facilitate the reprise of economic activity through the restoration of key routes into areas that were cut off.

It also aimed to save a few economic assets in danger of total collapse (e.g., bridges). In addition, the project demonstrated streamlined procurement and other managerial techniques that were more broadly applied in the administration of the government of Kenya.

PROJECT DESCRIPTION

The project consisted of four components: rural water supply, rural roads and bridges, rural health facilities, and urban roads.

The urban roads component was funded by the reallocation of credit proceeds under the Urban Transport Infrastructure Project. The Kenyan government and the International Development Association expected further funding to become available from outside sources to cover the funding gap (approximately $50 million in base costs).

PROJECT IMPLEMENTATION

The project was implemented by the Project Management Unit (PMU), a special unit of the Office of the President. Its governance was assured through oversight by a steering committee comprising the nine permanent secretaries of the interested ministries, the project manager, and his two advisors. The steering committee approved the annual program of work and the PMU budget associated with it, and it approved as well substantial amendments to that program as a result of interaction with the local disaster committees. It also set binding guidelines for the PMU's day-to-day management of the program; these guidelines were formally handed to and accepted by the PMU in the form of a manual of procedures mandated by the steering committee.

The project manager regularly reported his activities in a specific and agreed-upon format to the steering committee including all contract awards he made and handled on its behalf as well as disputes and other problems arising from the contracting and carrying out of the work. In the latter half of 1999, a decision to evaluate ENEP's performance and achievements was made. This evaluation was to be of three levels.

Level 1 involved the following.

- evaluation of actual project outputs for physical facilities to establish the contract baseline, verify outputs to address project objects, and justify duration against outputs
- evaluation of quality of structures and facilities: establish the damage done on infrastructure and facilities, verify that design had been professionally carried out, report on quality and standard of civil works and technical units' supervision, and establish that works as constructed addressed project objectives.

The above studies were contracted out to the University of Nairobi.

Levels 2 and 3 were studies to establish the effectiveness of the intervention and social impacts and whether the project was sustainable. Level 2, which involved assessment of effectiveness (i.e., analysis of attainment of project objectives), was awarded to Far-Mark Technovators. I was a director and key consultant on this assignment, which was to establish whether the ENEP effects and outcomes addressed project objectives to achieve the expected social impacts.

Level 3 involved an assessment of social impacts, which used indicators that related usage to outcomes and domain characteristics as follows.

1. Health
a. reduced disease prevalence
b. improved health environment within reasonable distance availed

2. Water
a. improved water quality
b. developed adequate potable water
c. improved physical access to water

3. Roads
a. socioeconomic activities restored
b. increased mobility in pursuit of socioeconomic services

Level 3 was also contracted out to Far-Mark Technovators as well.

TASKS OF THE ENEP SOCIAL IMPACT ASSESSMENT ASSIGNMENT

The specific objectives were as follows.

- Undertake a baseline survey to establish benchmarks against which the project's targets and actual impacts would be measured.
- Develop a community project monitoring system.
- Evaluate the social impact of the ENEP.

The social impact assignment deliverables included the following.

- an inception report
- a baseline survey report
- a participatory monitoring and evaluation system report
- an ENEP social-impact assessment report

Outputs of the inception report were as follows.

- a study methodology, which was used in the baseline survey report and the ENEP social impact assessments reports
- definitions of the key concepts
- defined social parameters for the ENEP impact assessment and unpacked tasks of the assignment for clarity and translation of ENEP's objectives into social issues

During the field visits, the consultants used the social issues identified above to dialogue with the stakeholders and establish benchmarks. The benchmarks were later used to develop appropriate data collection instruments.

BASELINE SURVEY AND BENCHMARK REPORT

The consulting team visited and collected pre– and post–El Niño data from the sampled forty-six subprojects. Data was analyzed to generate and index benchmarks and the output summarized by subsectors.

PARTICIPATORY MONITORING AND EVALUATION SYSTEM REPORT

The consultant designed a participatory monitoring and evaluation (PM&E) system for community-owned and -managed projects in the health and water subsectors to ensure the following.

- accountability and transparency of the management to the community and of the community with project sponsors
- enhanced ownership of the project by communities
- sustainability of community development projects
- enhanced capacity building in the management of community-owned and -managed projects.

  The output of these deliverables included among other things the following.

- a management checklist for a model water project incorporating the PM&E reporting format
- subsector monitoring reporting formats
- benchmarks/standards to assess level of community participation for sustainability and environmental mitigation in the health and water subsectors, which were developed by the consultant working in collaboration with the stakeholders. This exercise was not applicable to the road subsector as communities do not currently own or manage roads unlike the case with health and water facilities.

ENEP IMPACT ASSESSMENT REPORT

Far-Mark Technovators visited the subprojects and collected and analyzed ENEP intervention to generate pre– and post–El Niño benchmark indices. Differential values before, during, and after El Niño periods were computed as milestones to measure progress toward achievements of ENEP objectives and impacts on the beneficiary communities. The highlights of the achievement of objectives and social impacts to communities included the following.

Health Subsector

ENEP intervention improved the environment under which health care services were delivered.

Water Subsector

The outcomes were as follows.

- increased volume of potable water
- reduced travel distance and workload by women and girls
- reduction in the prevalence of waterborne diseases
- an improved living environment

Road Subsector

The outcomes were as follows.

- Essential social economic services, such as transportation of agricultural inputs and produce, were restored.
- Motorized transport of goods and services was restored.
- Motorized commuter services were restored.

The study revealed that communities were not economically empowered to utilize the restored social services and infrastructure. For optimal utilization of these facilities by the beneficiary communities, the study recommended the following.

- revitalize the economic activities, especially in rural areas
- introduce appropriate health insurance schemes
- facilitate the communities' access to relevant inputs including information

- train communities in management skills

SPECIAL ASSISTANCE FOR PROJECT IMPLEMENTATION (SAPI) FUNDED BY JICA (JAPAN INTERNATIONAL COOPERATION ASSISTANCE). THE PROJECT: HORTICULTURAL PRODUCING FACILITIES PROJECT UNDER HCDA (HORTICULTURAL CROPS DEVELOPMENT AUTHORITY)

The SAPI study was commissioned to detail how best to implement the JICA-funded horticultural producing facilities under HCDA. The project's aim was to construct precooling storages in the horticulture-producing (French beans, cut flowers, etc.) areas in Kenya and a cold-storage and auction center near the Nairobi International Airport to decrease postharvest losses and enhance the quality of the produce. Precooling facilities were to be established and built at satellite depots in Nkubu, Mwea, Sagana, Yatta, Machakos, Kibwezi, and Limuru.

The farmers' component was to spell out recommendations for the optimal organization for a sustainable horticultural project. The study therefore looked at the following.

- It took stock of existing marketing farmer groups in the project area and the key constraints to the formation and operation of marketing groups.
- It reviewed ongoing government development programs for farmers' organizations and of their work progress.
- Got a snapshot look at the rural social conditions in the project area in terms of the following.
  i. social organizations and group action
  ii. gender issues, especially changing roles of women in society and possible impacts on the proposed project
  iii. conducted a workshop on farmers' organizations at each depot, the objectives of which were as follows.
     - sensitizing the farmers to the proposed HCDA horticultural handling facilities and marketing arrangements
     - providing the farmers an opportunity to articulate their marketing problems and concerns

- exploring the basis for a collaborative relationship between farmers' marketing groups and HCDA under the proposed horticultural handling facilities and marketing arrangements
- supporting the setup of the distribution system (including the auction center) and its efficient operation
- analyzing the impact on the financial position of the executing agency

Recommendations from the workshops included the following.

- HCDA depot management should provide a grader/inspector at each collection point who would work with the groups' clerk/grader.
- A production and production collection program should be worked out as agreed by farmers' groups and should not be changed abruptly without discussion with farmers.
- HCDA should insure produce in transit to the depot and then to the national handling center.
- HCDA should recover its handling expenses on the basis of an agreed percentage of the realized auction value of the produce.
- HCDA should undertake to inform the marketing group of the results of the auction on a timely and regular basis.
- HCDA should remit produce payment within one to two weeks.
- Payment should be made by check or bank transfer.
- HCDA should arrange for inputs procurement on credit and ensure that all inputs (seed, agrochemicals) are of high quality.
- HCDA should provide new planting materials in relation to market requirements (specifically flowers).
- HCDA should provide the groups with training on production techniques for postharvest handling and grading on a regular basis.

The SAPI report on farmers' organizations recommended a plan that had the objective of realizing functional marketing groups with the capacity to produce the following desirable results.

- signing a collaborative contract with HCDA

- establishing a collection point for horticultural produce
- developing and implementing a production and marketing plan
- giving due consideration to generally acceptable agricultural practices
- maintaining good transaction records as well as books of account and paying members their dues promptly
- holding regular consultation meetings (committee and ordinary members) including elections
- making regular contact with potential support agencies (HCDA, MOARD, et al.) with the aim of enhancing groups' production and marketing performance

To implement this plan, the HCDA was largely responsible for undertaking a range of activities that included the following.

- Establish an extension support team at the depot level.
- Provide appropriate training to the depot extension team particularly in the area of participatory approaches, community mobilization, and group management.
- Create awareness of HCDA handling facilities in the catchment area of respective depots with special emphasis on areas with significant production potential (significant irrigation water, good soil, appropriate climate, and good access roads).
- Promote the formation of new marketing groups in areas with significant potential and subsequently update the marketing group list and map.
- Train marketing groups in general and in financial management with the aim of building their capacity for sustained operations.
- Establish a working relationship between marketing groups and respective depot management by availing support services.
- Training on a regular basis in the following areas.
  - horticultural production including safe use of fertilizers and other agrochemicals
  - postharvest handling and grading
  - group record keeping, compilation of accounts, and general management of the group

- o production planning within a group and among a cluster of groups
- o procurement of farm inputs including alternative sourcing of input credit
- o reliable and timely collection of horticultural produce from collection points to the precooling depot

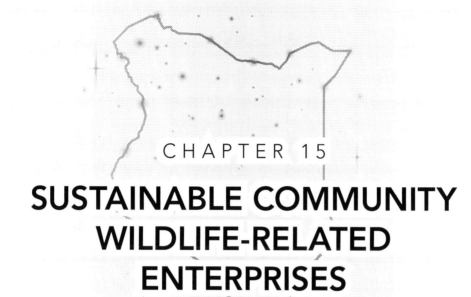

CHAPTER 15

SUSTAINABLE COMMUNITY WILDLIFE-RELATED ENTERPRISES

This assignment documented lessons learned in three community wildlife sanctuaries (Namunyak, Eselenkei, and Kimana) that were developed under the Conservation of Biodiverse Resource Management (COBRA) project. The major lesson learned confirmed that the key prerequisites for sustainability were these.

- a transparent election of officials in management and supervisory committees with bylaws to define the powers of the committee and ordinary membership
- hiring qualified staff based on criteria established and agreed upon prior to hiring
- designing management, accounting, and financial control systems for each enterprise
- implementing these systems and training staff on them
- equitably distributing the benefits from the enterprise

The COBRA project was the result of intensive interaction between USAID (United States Agency for International Development) and the Kenya Wildlife Service (KWS) as they sought to define the framework within which a community wildlife service or program would develop and operate with particular emphasis on a framework for sharing revenues and other benefits.

COBRA provided financial support for the Community Wildlife Service (CWS) for the period 1992–1997. The project was implemented through a $4.9 million contract involving a consortium of US-based organizations. The institutional contract was signed on December 17, 1992, and it ran through March 1998. The main contractor was Development Alternatives Inc. (DAI) with the African Wildlife Foundation (AWF) and Management Systems International (MSI) as subcontractors.

The goal of the COBRA project was to promote socioeconomic development through conservation and sustainable management of Kenya's natural resources. The goal was to benefit communities living adjacent to parks and reserves by the conservation and sustainable management of wildlife and natural resources through the following activities.

- establishing a functioning CWS unit with qualified and capable staff at headquarters and in the field
- developing human resources by supporting orientation and training in the KWS on new approaches to working with communities
- establishing a community and enterprise development fund aimed at supporting communities in community and enterprise development activities
- performing a studies, research, and policy analysis to assist the KWS in further defining key policy issues in wildlife-related management and utilization
- providing modest levels of commodity assistance (e.g., vehicles, motorbikes, microcomputers, and software) to help support the CWS headquarters and the field units' capacity to coordinate, implement, and monitor the COBRA project and the Community Wildlife Program.

The underlying philosophy behind the COBRA project was that the KWS could work directly and indirectly with target communities to demonstrate that wildlife had economic value that could benefit local communities and that wildlife could pay for itself in various ways.

The pilot wildlife-use rights program operating in Laikipia, Machakos, and Nakuru Districts was a clear demonstration of how in some places communities that had wildlife on their private land could earn money through their own enterprises on a long-term, sustainable basis. Indeed, pilot activities demonstrated that wildlife-use rights whether tourism related as in the case of the three community sanctuaries or consumptive[26] utilization of wildlife could provide benefits and that such activities strengthened communities' abilities to be meaningful partners in the business of conservation.

The COBRA project paper and the project agreement made provision for a community Enterprise Development Fund (EDF) to be administered by the CWS unit under the direction of the KWS management in consultation with USAID. The EDF would be used to assist communities living in wildlife dispersal areas to set up wildlife-related enterprises to generate income and employment opportunities thereby providing tangible economic benefits to the communities living with wildlife.

In 1994, the revenue-sharing scheme that arose from a commitment of the KWS director to share up to 25 percent of the revenue generated by protected areas with adjacent communities living along dispersal areas was merged with EDF funds and became the Benefit Sharing/Wildlife for Development Fund. The merger of the two funds resulted in several negative outcomes including the following.

- confusion between what constituted revenue sharing and enterprise support among communities

---

[26] Consumptive utilization of wildlife refers to culling wildlife for human consumption. Usually, Kenya Wildlife Service (KWS) would approve the culling of wildlife after a landowner has taken a census of the animals on his or her land supervised by KWS personnel.

- a culture of entitlement in some areas arising from the aforementioned confusion and resulting in pressure for projects to be financed even if they were potentially not viable
- concentration on social projects more than on enterprise initiatives because most officers were more comfortable (as were the communities) with proposing the former than they were the latter.

The above findings are underscored by the following partial figures.

- Between 1995 and 1997, about KES 63 million was allocated under the Wildlife for Development Fund (WDF) to community projects. Out of this amount,
  - 57.3 percent went to social projects such as bursaries; water development; and construction of schools, health centers, roads, and teachers' houses,
  - 24.6 percent went to capacity-building activities such as feasibility studies, registration of associations, security, training, equipment, seminars, and study tours, and
  - 18.3 percent went to enterprises such as boats, cultural *manyattas* (homestead of a Maasai), beehives, construction of bandas,[27] and tree nurseries.

The COBRA project had problems in retaining the services of an enterprise development specialist (EDS). The longest-serving one lasted two years, 1994–1996. The inability to keep an EDS during project implementation left the WDF without any consistent oversight. It took nearly four years to develop a set of WDF guidelines that the main parties could agree on. These guidelines served mainly to allow committees at the director, department, and field levels to select social and economic projects but did not provide guidance for communities, NGOs, or other would-be partners for identifying the appropriate type of projects. There was too much reliance on KWS field personnel to put together a proposal. The guidelines sufficed for KWS's purpose of having rational project criteria, but it

---

[27] Bandas are tourist facilities constructed using local materials, usually trees cut from the neighborhood.

failed to provide partners the support necessary for project identification and development.

The COBRA program covered the following focal areas.

- eastern Kenya (Samburu, Isiolo)
- mountain areas (Laikipia, Mount Kenya)
- southern Kenya (Kajiado)
- coastal areas (the north and south coasts)

The constraints to effective implementation of the COBRA project included among others the following things.

- the assumption that communities had the capacity to implement successful enterprises in the community wildlife sanctuaries
- the fact that the KWS was an evolving organization and was nervous about working with partners in the implementation of the sanctuaries
- the assumption that the private sector would move in to develop tourist facilities in the sanctuaries
- the assumption that communities had the capacity to understand projects that fostered tourism

Among the projects assisted under COBRA at different levels were the Namunyak, Eselenkei, and Kimana wildlife sanctuaries, which have been used as samples for this case study, whose focus is on lessons learned about the establishment, development, and implementation of community wildlife sanctuaries.

FIELD DISCUSSIONS

Field discussions and interviews with various stakeholders took place on the following topics.

- the wildlife enterprises, community-based organization (CBO)/sanctuary started under or as a result of COBRA

- inputs provided by COBRA
- original expectations of the local stakeholders and whether these were met
- what worked well and what did not and why

The findings entail the key lessons learned from the establishment of community sanctuaries under the COBRA project. The lessons learned are grouped into eight subheadings as follows.

- security of land tenure
- the need to work in strategic partnerships
- the need for accountability and transparency in the management of community benefits from the sanctuary
- benefits to communities/landowners
- the need for long-term support to establish sanctuaries
- building on traditional governance and knowledge
- training and transfer of skills
- marketing strategies

CONCLUSIONS FROM THE FINDINGS AND LITERATURE REVIEW

Ownership and management of sanctuaries and the enterprises should be unlinked for optimal results. When the community managed the Kimana sanctuary, it was difficult to account for benefits from the sanctuary. In most cases, local owners did not have the skills to market the sanctuary.

The deals between developers and the communities gave developers exclusive rights for long periods thus denying the local communities opportunities to negotiate with other developers.

In the three sanctuaries discussed here, community contributions were minimal, with Namunyak providing labor to reconstruct the burned-down mess of the Sarara camp. Kimana and Eselenkei members contributed only their portions of land where the sanctuaries were situated. As in other types of businesses, minimal contributions to equity imply minimal returns in the form of dividends. This is possibly why the members of the three sanctuaries did not negotiate for higher returns from the tourist activities in the sanctuaries.

Sanctuaries located where opportunity costs for land use were high negotiated better returns with private developers. An example is Kimana, where lease money paid to the community was KES 200,000 per month followed by Eselenkei at an annual lease of KES 350,000 per annum. The opportunity cost for land in Namunyak was almost zero as members of the two group ranches grazed their livestock in the ranches without restriction.

Mentors, investors, and donors to community sanctuaries should dissuade the beneficiaries from investing in activities that are incompatible with conservation. For example, Kimana was contributing KES 4,500,000 toward the survey of two-acre plots for its members on the Namelok side of the Kimana group ranch. Agricultural activity is incompatible with conservation in that such activities increase human-wildlife conflict in an area.

The setting aside of land for the establishment of the Kimana and Eselenkei sanctuaries helped maintain wildlife dispersal areas for Amboseli and keeping clear the corridor between Amboseli, Chyullu, and the Tsavos. The establishment of the Namunyak sanctuary was within the Matthews Range habitat for the elephants and a migratory route for elephants from Mount Kenya, Rumuruti, and the Aberdares. The findings show an increase of awareness of conservation and a change of attitude toward wildlife among the local people.

In all cases, there were problems with sharing the benefits from the sanctuaries. A clear benefit-sharing policy needed to be developed and implemented in all sanctuaries. One of the recommended ways was to set up a trust where all the payments would be remitted by the developer. Trustees appointed from a wide base would be entrusted with the distribution of the benefits to the beneficiaries.

GOLINI-MWALUGANJE ELEPHANT SANCTUARY

The community-owned Golini-Mwaluganje Elephant Sanctuary, in the Kwale District of Kenya's Coastal Province just forty-five kilometers southwest of Mombasa, was one of the initial beneficiaries of the COBRA project.. The sanctuary has an area of thirty-six square kilometers, and it and the adjacent Shimba Hills National Reserve combine to form the Shimba Hills ecosystem. The sanctuary was formed in the early 1990s as a cooperative project between the people of the surrounding Mwaluganje community, USAID, the Born Free

Foundation, and the Eden Wildlife Trust. The local community set aside land to be converted to an elephant sanctuary from which they could derive benefits from entry fees and thereby conserve wildlife.

THE MWALUGANJE ELEPHANT SANCTUARY ATTRACTIONS

Elephants' Experience

Elephants are the main attraction at the Mwaluganje Elephant Sanctuary; there are as many as 150 there. It has been historically a bull area where independent elephant bulls grow in preparation for the demanding life of being breeding males. Their families live in the neighboring Shimba Hills Reserve and the Mwaluganje Forest.

On occasion, family groups visit males during the mating season or cross the sanctuary as they travel between feeding areas. Once or twice a year, several related elephant families travel as a unit of two hundred females and calves of all ages. They gather in the Shimba Hills and move into the Mwaluganje Elephant Sanctuary during the rainy season, December and March–April. Such large herds usually stay for no longer than three to four days and are consequently a rare and magnificent sight. As with human family reunions, these gatherings are marked by noisy greetings such as trumpeting.

Botanical Experience

Dinosaur cycads are fanlike plants that evolved around 300 million years ago can be sighted while driving across the Mwaluganje Elephant Sanctuary. They were most plentiful during the Jurassic period (180 million years ago), when dinosaurs roamed the earth. All six of Kenya's cycad species (*Eucephalartos hildebrantii*) are found in Mwaluganje. This species can grow to be 150 years old. Today's cycads are confined to tropical and subtropical regions. There are eleven genera and approximately 250 species. The second largest is the African family, the *Eucephalartos*, which consists of 60 species.

Baobab Trees

Mwaluganje Elephant Sanctuary's baobab trees (*Adansonia digitata*) are one of Africa's most unusual deciduous trees. The interior of the baobab's trunk (reaching up to nine meters or thirty feet in diameter) and the lower branches are soft and spongy and can store large quantities of water. Baobabs are specially adapted for long dry seasons. They are leafless during this time of year thus reducing transpiration or water loss. The baobab is an extremely slow-growing tree reaching up to eighteen meters (sixty feet) in height. Truly giant specimens may be several thousand years old. Bats pollinate the flowers of the baobab, and many other animals depend on the unique tree for food and shelter. There are plenty in the Mwaluganje Elephant Sanctuary.

The Scenic Landscape

The Mwaluganje Elephant Sanctuary valleys overlooking the Shimba Hills are a sight to behold. With quiet flowing waters and serene surroundings, it is like a paradise. These beautiful hills roll up to Tsavo National Park to the east and the Indian Ocean to the west, and they are marked by striking features including the Golini Cliffs, Kitanze Falls, and Manolo River, which consists of riverine vegetation and meandering rivers.

Educational Experience

The Mwaluganje Elephant Sanctuary was launched in the early 1990s largely to reduce local human-elephant conflicts, which were on the rise due to a greater number of elephants and people; elephants would destroy crops, and people would retaliate. More than two hundred families have voluntarily contributed land to the reserve agreeing not to farm this important elephant habitat.

Today, these families live nearby and manage the sanctuary; they earn more from tourism than from farming, a critical factor in ensuring the survival of these elephants. The sanctuary has also enabled the community to build schools and enjoy a steady water supply and better roads.

The Mwaluganje Elephant Sanctuary is currently receiving support from Eden Wildlife Trust, Born Free Foundation, East African Wildlife Society, and Pact, Inc. to build the community's capacity to run the sanctuary in a sustainable way for the benefit of present and future generations. There is a growing consensus that the best way to encourage local communities to protect wildlife and natural habitats is to enable local communities to benefit from the existence and use of these natural resources. For example, in the case of elephants, Urs Kreuter and Randy Simmons concluded, [28]

Community conservation in Zimbabwe has had its successes. Zimbabwe's Communal Areas Management Program for Indigenous Resources (CAMPFIRE) is the most often mentioned African community conservation effort. Community conservation in Kenya is not well-known, but it has also been relatively successful. Since 1992, USAID has been funding the COBRA project to assist the Kenya Wildlife Service in developing and implementing a strategy for working with communities who live with wildlife on their lands. With COBRA assistance, KWS has carried out dozens of small-scale community projects, such as construction or rehabilitation of clinics and schools and construction of water troughs and cattle dips. But the most interesting and promising initiatives have been the identification and implementation of income-generating projects whose success is directly linked to the well-being of wildlife. The Golini-Mwaluganje Community Elephant Sanctuary is a relatively successful community conservation project poised for even greater successes, and though it is plagued by unresolved elephant management problems,

It provides a good case study for COBRA projects that demonstrate that communities will participate in conservation when they can reap benefits from it.[29]

---

[28] Urs Kreuter and Randy Simmons wrote, "There is a growing consensus that the best way to encourage local communities to protect wildlife and natural habitats is to enable local communities to benefit from the existence and use of these natural resources."

[29] This comes from a paper written by Cochiba and Ndiangu, https://dlc.dlib.indiana.edu/dlc/handle/10535/1957.

KIMANA COMMUNITY WILDLIFE SANCTUARY

The Kimana Community Wildlife Sanctuary was funded partly by the COBRA project. Other partners included the European Union, which donated money for a sixty-one-kilometer game-proof fence that was put up around the western edge of the Amboseli National Park (ANP) in 1997, the Friends of Conservation, and the Amboseli Community Wildlife Project (ACWP), which helped in planning, designing, and organizing the construction of the required infrastructure including the gates, purchase of uniforms, and acquisition of entrance-ticket books. Specific activities funded under the COBRA project included the following.

- developing a business plan for a wildlife sanctuary
- providing educational seminars for the Kimana group ranch committee to sensitize them to benefits of a community wildlife sanctuary
- providing educational tours for the Kimana group ranch committee to the Maasai Mara and the Laikipia ranches to learn the benefits accruing to communities from wildlife
- developing infrastructure in the sanctuary to the tune of KES 4.2 million including road network, a toilet block, and staff housing
- training seventeen community game rangers and seven community wildlife scouts

Let us now look at the Kimana Community Wildlife Sanctuary in the Kimana Tikondo group ranch.

KIMANA TIKONDO GROUP RANCH

The Kimana Tikondo group ranch (25,120 ha) is at the base of the northern foothills of Mount Kilimanjaro and adjacent to the Amboseli National Park in the newly created Loitokitok District in the Rift Valley of Kenya. Formerly owned jointly by some 845 extended families of the indigenous IIkisonko Maasai pastoralists, the ranch has recently been subdivided into small and individually owned plots and ranches.

Large sections of the ranch are arid, but there are a number of wetlands including the Kimana swamp, which is fed by the Kimana and Tikondo streams. These swamps are the main sources of permanent water in a region that receives low and unpredictable rainfall (ranging between 300 mm and 500 mm annually). These swamps and the vegetation around them were traditionally, for the local Maasai pastoralists one of their most important dry-season livestock grazing and watering refuges and were sources of food, firewood, building materials, craft materials, and medicine.

The Kimana group ranch is also a very important dispersal area and seasonal migration corridor for wildlife between the Amboseli National Park and the Tsavo National Park. Because of the availability of permanent sources of water, the Kimana group ranch offers opportunities for livestock herders, agriculturalists (the majority of them recent migrants), and wild animals.

However, as a result of competition for scarce range resources including water and pasture, serious conflicts often erupt between these user groups that threatens their welfare and well-being as well as the area's biodiversity.

The individualization of land tenure has exacerbated these conflicts as the titleholders fragment their land and sell or lease those portions to Maasai elites and non-Maasai people. The new owners immediately fence and convert these lands into commercial beef or arable land and sometimes tourist areas or for other uses.

This hasty sale of land and the resultant loss of access and user rights over critical livelihood resources have driven many Maasai into landlessness and poverty. Whereas the Maasai are denied the opportunity to access the natural resources in the park, wildlife in the park often forage on their lands, spread diseases to livestock, damage crops, and endanger livestock and human lives. As a result, Maasai resentment toward wildlife conservation and tourism development has been on the increase. The negative attitudes are accentuated by the fact that the local Maasai pastoralists receive very few direct benefits from the revenues generated from conservation and tourism in their territory but are the ones who bear most of the costs of wildlife; the costs of not using land for traditional activities accrues entirely to them.

Exclusion from critical natural resources in the park essential for livestock production has had profound negative effects on the Maasai including growing poverty and a breakdown in the social systems of livestock sharing and exchange. As a consequence, the Maasai have become overwhelmingly hostile to the park and unsympathetic to its wildlife.

There is a claim that in protest and frustration, the Maasai started to spear wild animals. As a result, Kenya's wildlife has been increasingly suffering major depletion. As a result of increased human-wildlife conflicts, poaching, and complications brought about by the subdivision of the group ranches around the Amboseli National Park, the government came to the realization that the future survival of the more than 75 percent of Kenya's wild animals that lived seasonally or permanently outside the park depended on the goodwill of the local Maasai pastoralists. The subdivision, fencing, and conversion of Maasai group ranches into privately owned farmlands was a threat to not only wildlife but also to the tourism industry, which depended on it.

Subsequently, in 1990, a major policy shift occurred when the newly formed Kenya Wildlife Service (KWS) started to encourage and aid the Maasai to participate in conservation through the establishment of locally owned, small-scale wildlife-based ecotourism projects as a form of commercial enterprise. Ecotourism was viewed as a viable tool not only to curb further wildlife losses but also to reconcile the otherwise intractable conflicts between conservation and development.

The assumption was that active local involvement in wildlife management and tourism benefits would provide economic alternatives that would ultimately relieve the day-to-day pressures that subsistence livelihoods placed on conservation efforts. Subsequently, a growing number of the local pastoralists struggling for survival amid declining livestock production are increasingly turning to wildlife-based ecotourism to supplement their livelihoods and to spur development in their homelands. One of the best-known and pioneering examples of wildlife-based ecotourism initiatives in Kenya is the Kimana Community Wildlife Sanctuary (KCWS).

Initially, there was a lot of resistance in the community because its members had negative attitudes toward wildlife and tourism. The local Maasai community thought that the KWS was going to take away its land as it had with Amboseli; they feared they would lose access to the water and pasture resources in the Kimana swamp. They also thought they were not going to benefit from the proposed sanctuary because tourism was a white man's business and for just a few rich individuals. Still another challenge was that they thought of tourism only in the national park. So the general feeling was that if they accepted the sanctuary project, then the Amboseli National Park would be extended into the Kimana group ranch.

In an effort to convince the local people that the project was designed to benefit them, the KWS arranged for and sponsored a small number of influential community leaders and elders to do a study tour of successful community wildlife conservation projects in other parts of the country. The findings of the study were reported and deliberated upon in a group ranch meeting. In the meeting, the leaders convinced members that communities in other wildlife areas were benefitting from tourist activities. The project was slowly accepted after the community was assured that the government had no designs on their land and that they would own the project.

The major motivation for the members to accept and support a wildlife sanctuary in their midst, however, was the desire to receive economic benefits. Each of the member families was promised an annual dividend paid from the entrance fees, the lease fees from the three campsites and one game lodge in the sanctuary, and a certain percentage of tourist bed nights. Some money could also be retained for joint community development projects such as schools and dispensaries and a revolving loan scheme.

While the concept of local participation in community-based wildlife conservation and tourism development was novel and strange, the possibility of making money was enthusiastically welcomed. In fact, without the promise of money, a community wildlife sanctuary would not have made sense to the people of Kimana, whose main source of livelihood—livestock production— depended heavily on the swamp. With the promise of money on the horizon, the KCWS was born. This marked the first time that the Maasai were drawn into developing conservation-oriented tourism. When the people trusted that they were going to benefit, the project got underway.

Funds for the project were provided by several international donors including USAID, the World Bank, and the Kenyan government. In addition to these donors, a large number of other stakeholders including conservation-oriented

NGOs, researchers, and volunteers provided infrastructural, material, and technical support.

The sanctuary negotiated a deal with a private tour operator to build a luxury lodge in the sanctuary and attract tourists. The neighboring lodges, the Kilimanjaro Buffalo (now the Amboseli Sopa Lodge) and the Kimana Lodge, both owned by the Kilimanjaro Safari Club together with the three leased tented camps in the sanctuary were to assist in marketing the resort internationally. Additional overseas exposure and marketing was provided by a BBC documentary recorded in the sanctuary. For the local market, marketing was done by Abercrombie and Kent under a commission arrangement with the sanctuary.

The sanctuary had a tremendous advantage in terms of marketing thanks to its proximity to the ANP. The entry fee into the sanctuary was fixed at $10 per person, which was considerably lower than the $27 per person charged by the ANP at that time. It was anticipated that lower entrance fees would attract visitors from the ANP. When the sanctuary opened its doors for business in February 1996, it attracted an overwhelming amount of local and international media coverage as it was the first genuinely community-owned and -run wildlife sanctuary in East Africa.

In recognition of its significance to the country's conservation efforts, the Kenyan government and international organizations hired the Royal Ballet to perform at the sanctuary's opening ceremony. For its pioneering and exemplary work in community-based wildlife conservation, the sanctuary was granted the prestigious Silver Otter award by the British Guild of Travel Writers in 1996, the first time Kenya had ever received such an award.

The sanctuary's success stories were told around the globe, and the future looked even more promising especially for the people of Kimana. The sanctuary was locally perceived as one of the biggest and most significant developments in the history of Kimana so much so that it formed a dividing line between the past and the present. Even today, 1996 is remembered as the landmark year for the Maasai community's involvement in wildlife tourism.

Shortly after its official opening, the sanctuary began attracting tourists, and it hosted eight hundred visitors during its first year. The people of Kimana were amazed to see tourists flock to the sanctuary. Many villagers could not believe that this same old wetland they had grown up with and took for granted had become their future. Tourism was something they had watched since the ANP had been created, but they had not been directly involved with it in any way. People could have never guessed that tourists would pay money to visit Kimana. When someone asked residents, "Did you believe that tourists would ever come and pay to see animals in your ranch?" the common reply was, "We honestly didn't know that could happen."

Within a short period, Kimana put itself on the international tourist map, and tourists quickly became acquainted with the sanctuary apparently unaware of the latent controversies that surrounded its establishment or the larger political and ecological context in which tourism and conservation in Amboseli were situated.

In spite of the initial opposition, the people of Kimana overwhelmingly and enthusiastically threw their support behind the sanctuary. Many villagers started to exhibit positive attitudes toward wildlife and tourism. Instead of spearing wild animals, they protected them as a valuable economic asset that needed everybody's care.

Everything looked promising for the inhabitants of the Kimana group ranch particularly as tourists continued to flock to the sanctuary; it had a unique appeal of its own. Walking around the sanctuary was not only a natural experience but also a cultural one given that a cultural boma[30] at the edge of the sanctuary satisfied the needs of tourists interested in Maasai lifestyles. Instead of competing with the national park, the sanctuary complemented it well.

Generally, the motivation behind the establishment of the community sanctuary was the government's quest to protect and conserve the fragile wildlife resources of the ANP. Community participation in income-generating opportunities in tourism was just a bait to achieve conservation goals. In spite of the project being conceived by the KWS, many local Maasai strongly believe that it was they who initiated the project. In any case, they are the recognized owners of the sanctuary.

---

[30] A boma is a homestead of the Maasai designed as a tourist facility so visitors can experience houses and homes in which local people live.

INFRASTRUCTURAL DEVELOPMENTS

The KWS pledged KES 6 million, and the remainder of the money was to come from the sanctuary's profits. Although the KWS financed infrastructural developments in the sanctuary to the tune of KES 4.2 million, this was far below what it had pledged. Relative to the initially projected annual earnings based on estimated financial investment costs, the capital spent and the time needed to begin profitable operations were considerably underestimated. This gap and the other financial and accounting confusions resulted in negative repercussions for the villagers and their relationship with the group ranch committee (GRC) and foreign investors. The sanctuary's budgetary deficits were attributed to lack of transparency and accountability in the group ranch's leadership.

While the money collected from entrance fees by the community game scouts was handed over to the group ranch treasurer, nobody in the community knew how these funds were spent. This money, KES 1 million the first year, was supposed to be put in a bank account and then distributed to members at the end of every year minus management costs.

Over and above that, the group ranch was to be paid a certain share of the nightly bed lodging rate received from tourists. This fee per visitor per night was supposed to be invested in the construction of a school and clinic, support other special community projects, and run a small, soft-loans scheme for members. The GRC was censured not only for being secretive and dishonest but also for running the sanctuary as its personal property. It was difficult for the villagers to comprehend the income generated by the sanctuary because of the high operating costs deducted from it. The people of Kimana could see foreign tourists stay at the campsites and lodge in their sanctuary, but no profits in terms of direct dividends were forthcoming as had been expected and promised.

The community complained that the only local people who had so far claimed any profit from the sanctuary were a few elites many of whom were wealthy and politically powerful members of the community. Otherwise, a huge chunk of the sanctuary's tourism revenue was garnered by foreign investors, tour operators, middlemen, and the government.

In conclusion, ecotourism, if cautiously designed and managed, can provide a sustainable return much of which can be retained in a community and thus contribute to development. However, for local participation in wildlife-based ecotourism development in Kimana to succeed, issues that relate to local ownership, equitable benefit sharing, good governance, and political control over access and user rights to land resources need to be more carefully addressed.

There is also an urgent need to develop local capacity particularly in the fields of management and business skills. Training especially in leadership and microenterprises management skills will ultimately equip the Maasai with sufficient business expertise to negotiate equitable and sustainable relationships with other actors and agencies in ecotourism development and undertake collective action in natural resource management.

THE IL NGWESI COMMUNITY WILDLIFE SANCTUARY

The Il Ngwesi Community Wildlife Sanctuary is another example of a sustainable wildlife project. A business plan created by a financial consultant demonstrated that developing tourist facilities at Il Ngwesi group ranch and marketing the product along with the neighboring Lewa Downs would generate great rewards for the community in the form of jobs and financial returns and promote conservation. An update of the project done on April 4, 2016, gave the following account.

The Il Ngwesi Story

In 2016, Il Ngwesi was twenty years old. Supporting both communities and wildlife, it remains the only upmarket lodge that is both owned and run by the community. Its significance cannot be overstated. Its remarkable story is told here as it enters its third decade.

Neighboring Lewa, Borana, and Lekurruki, Il Ngwesi covers 16,500 hectares and is home to the Il Lakipiak Maasai—"people of wildlife." Truly special, this award-winning enterprise combines ecotourism with sustainable environmental management and community development.

Early Days

Following an approach by Ian Craig from neighboring Lewa Wildlife Conservancy in the mid-1990s, Il Ngwesi became the first Maasai group ranch in Laikipia to join Lewa on a conservation and community-development journey with a vision far beyond its borders. Community elders agreed to set aside 8,675 hectares of their grazing land for conservation, and in 1996, with funding from USAID through the Kenya Wildlife Service, the superb Il Ngwesi Eco-Lodge was built.

From the 80 men who worked for 10 months to build the lodge, 10 were selected to be trained to run the lodge and host tourists. A team of rangers (now totaling 16) was also trained at Lewa to oversee security, and monitor and protect people and wildlife.

Wildlife Returns

Wildlife numbers steadily increased. More elephants were evident almost immediately, and within five years numbers had grown significantly, as the elephants had found a safe place to rest and feed. With the exception of waterbuck, which were translocated, all other species native to the area recovered naturally, including the endangered Grevy's zebra, reticulated giraffe, and gerenuk (three of the "Northern Five"). In 2002, a rare black rhino male known as Omni, reared on Lewa after being born to a blind female, was translocated to a protected and fenced-in sanctuary close to the lodge. It was joined in 2006 by two white rhinos, also from Lewa. Tragically in 2013, Omni became a victim of rhino poaching, but the two white rhinos remain and the rangers watch over them night and day. All of the main predators, including lions, leopards, cheetahs, hyenas, and jackals, are now present in the group ranch.

The Model

Profits from the lodge, donations from well-wishers, and partnerships with local and international NGOs all support a range of community projects and, at the same time, ensure that the environment is managed sustainably. The model helps to foster communities that value wildlife and see purpose in acting as custodians of the land. Crucially, Il Ngwesi is one of thirty-three conservancies that are supported by the Northern Rangelands Trust (NRT) and that collectively cover 440,000 square kilometers. As well as providing a large and secure environment for wildlife populations to live and migrate to and from, the NRT supports communities in developing and benefiting from tourism. This managed landmass is particularly important for the conservation of endangered species, including the African lion, the African wild dog.

SHIMONI, MKWIRO, AND KIBUYUNI FISHERMEN PROJECT

The Shimoni, Mkwiro, and Kibuyuni Fishermen Project was a beneficiary of the COBRA project. While COBRA's main focus was support for communities adjacent to parks or communities living in wildlife areas, the coastal area was included as a special area. In the areas of terrestrial and marine conservation, conflicts exist as human beings and wildlife compete for similar resources. The KWS enforces conservation practices that include protection of biodiversity. Some of the activities carried out with COBRA funding on the coast included the education and sensitization of fishermen communities and an educational tour for the Shimoni, Mkwiro, and Kibuyuni fishermen to Zanzibar to learn sustainable fishing practices and how to cultivate commercial seaweed.

The livelihood of the Shimoni, Mkwiro, and Kibuyuni communities has traditionally been the fisheries' resources in the area. The community's fishing practices include spear fishing, ring-net fishing, line fishing, and trap and aquarium fishing. Neighboring this fishing area is the Kisite Mpunguti Marine National Park, whose fishing and other biodiversity resources are protected by the KWS. Let us look at this resource and learn how the gazettement of the Kisite Mpunguti National Park and Reserve has reduced fishing grounds for the communities there.

KISITE MPUNGUTI MARINE NATIONAL PARK AND RESERVE

Established in 1973, the Kisite Marine National Park is an area along Kenya's southern coast that has been free of fishing of any kind since the 1990s. The results are astonishing; in cooperation with Tanzania's Mtang'ata Collaborative Management Area, which is across the border and has outlawed destructive fishing practices, authorities have managed to increase fish stocks, reduce damage to coral, and maintain biodiversity even in areas not encompassed by the marine park. While some nice dive sites exist outside the park, those who have benefitted from the effects of protection the longest are within Kisite's boundaries. Here, the fish are more numerous and biodiversity is much greater.

The marine park is forty kilometers from Ukunda Town in Kenya's Msambweni District. The Kisite Park covers eleven square kilometers while Mpunguti Reserve covers twenty-eight square kilometers and includes four small islands surrounded by coral reef.

Kisite Island is a small, waterless coral island eight kilometers offshore in the marine park. Coral platforms around the raised central portion are exposed at low tide. The three other coral islets in the park, Mpunguti ya Juu, Mpunguti ya Chini, and Liwe la Jahazi, lie closer to the larger Wasini Island and are covered in scrub; they support no significant wildlife or birds. The surrounding waters have well-developed coral gardens and a large variety of fish. Marine life comprises about 250 recorded fish species including triggerfish, moray eels, angelfish, butterfly fish, groupers, parrot fish, wrasses, scorpion fish, puffer fish, damselfish, rays, snappers, green sea turtles, hawksbill turtles, 70 resident dolphins, over 140 catalogued sea turtles, seasonal humpback whales, whale sharks, 56 genera of coral, seagrass, gastropods, many seabirds in large nesting colonies, and an internationally significant number of roseate terns and crab plovers.

As the biodiversity resources continued to increase in the marine park and preserve, the fishing resources of the communities adjacent to the park were on the decline partly because of population increases and partly because of the use of small nets and other inappropriate fishing practices that killed small fish.

The training provided with funding from COBRA was designed to sensitize the local communities' conservation of the biodiversity in the Kisite Mpunguti National Park and Reserve while providing them with alternative sources of livelihood like seaweed farming and sustainable fishing practices.

ABOUT THE AUTHOR

John Makilya, a native of Kenya, has spent the bulk of his career working with communities to establish and implement sustainable community-owned enterprises. He is also the author of *Life Lessons of an Immigrant*.

NOTES

1 "World Economic Outlook Database, April 2019." IMF.org. International Monetary Fund. Retrieved 29 September 2019.

2 "World Bank Country and Lending Groups." datahelpdesk.worldbank.org. World Bank. Retrieved 29 September 2019.

3 "Population, total—Kenya." data.worldbank.org. World Bank. Retrieved 17 January 2020.

4 "World Economic Outlook Database, April 2019." IMF.org. International Monetary Fund. Retrieved 15 June 2019.

5 "Global Economic Prospects, January 2020: Slow Growth, Policy Challenges." PDF. openknowledge.worldbank.org. World Bank, 147. Retrieved 17 January 2020.

6 "The World Factbook." CIA.gov. Central Intelligence Agency. Retrieved 15 June 2019.

7 World poverty clock.

8 "Human Development Index (HDI)." hdr.undp.org. HDRO (Human Development Report Office), United Nations Development Programme. Retrieved 11 December 2019.

9 "Inequality-adjusted Human Development Index (IHDI)." hdr.undp.org. HDRO (Human Development Report Office), United Nations Development Programme. Retrieved 11 December 2019.

10 "Labor force, total—Kenya." data.worldbank.org. World Bank. Retrieved 17 January 2020.

11 "Employment to population ratio, 15+, total (%) (national estimate) - Kenya." data.worldbank.org. World Bank. Retrieved 17 January 2020.

12 Statista.

13 "Sessional-Paper-No-10(1965) African Socialism and its Application to Planning in Kenya." PDF. Tom Mboya and Mwai Kibaki-Kenya Government, 1965. Retrieved 30 September 2018.

14 "Sessional-Paper-No-10 (1965) African Socialism and its Application to Planning in Kenya pg 16,Relationship With Other Countries" (PDF). Kenya Government 1965. Retrieved 30 September 2018.

15 Mwangi S. Kimeny, Francis M. Mwega, Njuguna S. Ndung'u. (May 2016). "The African Lions: Kenya country case study." PDF. The Brookings Institution. Retrieved 23 May 2016.

16 Meilink, Henk A. (June 1982). "The effects of import-substitution: the case of Kenya's manufacturing sector." Nairobi: Institute for Development Studies, University of Nairobi. Retrieved 30 September 2018.

17 "Kenya (05/07/12)." U.S. Department of State. Retrieved 11 June 2015.

18 Greenhouse, Steven. (27 November 1991). "Aid Donors Insist on Kenya Reforms." *New York Times Archives*. Steven Greenhouse. Retrieved 30 September 2018.

19 "Sessional Paper no. 9, 2012 On The National Industrialization Policy Framework For Kenya." PDF; 11. Kenya Government. Retrieved 14 April 2019.

20 Rono, J. K. "The impact of the structural adjustment programmes on Kenyan society." *Journal of Social Development in Africa* 17, 81–98.

21 Kinyanjui, Mary Njeri. "Women and the informal economy in urban Africa: From the margins to the centre." Zed Books, 2014.

22 "Kenya Trade Liberalization of the 80s and 90s: Policies, Impacts, Implications." PDF. Geoffrey Gertz, Wolfensohn Center for Development, Brookings Institution. Retrieved 30 September 2018.

23 David Bigman (2002). "Globalization and the Developing Countries: Emerging Strategies for Rural Development and Poverty Alleviation." CABI, 136. ISBN 978-0-85199-575-5.

24 "Nairobi halts IMF and World Bank reforms." www.independent.co.uk. 24 March 1993. Retrieved 30 September 2018.

25 "Kenya: World Bank, IMF Suspend Financial Aid to Kenya." allafrica.com. Retrieved 30 September 2018.

26 "Economic Recovery Strategy For Wealth And Employment Creation 2003 - 2007." PDF. Kenya Government, 2003. Retrieved 30 September 2018.

27 "Kenya Vision 2030." PDF. Kenya Government, 2007. Retrieved 30 September 2018.

28 "The Impact of Election (2007/2008): Violence on Kenya's Economy: Lessons Learned?" PDF. Dr. Kiti Reginah, M.K Kitiabi. ke.boell.org. Retrieved 30 September 2018.

29 "Economic Survey 2018." Archived from the original on 30 September 2018. Retrieved 30 September 2018.

30 "Kenya After Kibaki." *New African Magazine*, 8 May 2012. Retrieved 24 March 2019.

31 "Kenya Overview 2013–2018." World Bank. Retrieved 30 September 2018.

32 "Kenya Economic Survey 2018." KNBS, Republic of Kenya, 25 April 2018. Retrieved 24 March 2019.

33 "KenInvest supports small businesses to become engines of growth in Kenya." dandc.eu. Archived 9 August 2011 at the Wayback Machine. Retrieved March 13, 2016.

34 "Kenya Economic Update: Kenya's Economy Poised to Rebound in 2018 and Remain Robust through 2020," PDF. World Bank, 11 October 2018. Retrieved 24 March 2019.

35 "2019 Budget Policy Statement." The National Treasury, Republic of Kenya, 11 February 2019. Retrieved 24 March 2019.

36 "The Draft 2019 Budget Policy Statement Note." PDF. Cytonn Kenya, 11 February 2019. Retrieved 24 March 2019.

37   Vision 2030. http://www.vision2030.go.ke/index.php. Archived 15 December 2012 at the Wayback Machine. Retrieved March 13, 2016.

38   "Archived copy." PDF. Archived from the original PDF on 6 June 2013. Retrieved 28 November 2012.

39   "The Economic Pillar." http://www.vision2030.go.ke/index.php/pillars. Archived 15 December 2012 at the Wayback Machine. Retrieved 25 November 2012.

40   "The Social Pillar." http://www.vision2030.go.ke/index.php/pillars/index/social. Archived 15 December 2012 at the Wayback Machine. Retrieved 25 November 2012.

41   "The Political Pillar." http://www.vision2030.go.ke/index.php/pillars/index/political. Archived 15 December 2012 at the Wayback Machine. Retrieved 26 November 2012.

42   Daniel Branch. 15 November 2011. "Kenya: Between Hope and Despair, 1963–2011". Yale University Press. ISBN 978-0-300-14876-3.

43   S. Nyamu. "Inflation Rates." www.centralbank.go.ke. Archived from the original on 16 October 2015. Retrieved 14 September 2015.

44   Kenya Inflation Rate. Archived copy. PDF. Archived from the original (PDF) on 13 November 2012. Retrieved 28 November 2012. Archived copy. Archived from the original on 16 October 2015. Retrieved 14 September 2015.

45   "Central Bank Of Kenya Set To Release Details Of New Look Currency This Week." The National Treasury, 8 August 2019. Retrieved 8 August 2019.

46   Kenya country profile. Library of Congress Federal Research Division (June 2007). This article incorporates text from this source, which is in the public domain.

47   Kenya   Budget.   http://www.pwc.com/ke/en/pdf/kenya-budget-2012-revenue-an d-expenditure-highlights.pdf.

48   "2018 Budget Policy Statement." The National Treasury, Republic of Kenya, 1 February 2018. Retrieved 24 March 2019.

49   "Effect of Public Debt on Economic Growth in Kenya." PDF. Gideon Ledama Kobey, University of Nairobi, 1 November 2016. Retrieved 24 March 2019.

50   "Where Will Our Money Go? Guide for Members of Parliament 2002." PDF. Institute of Economic Affairs, Kenya, 1 June 2001. Retrieved 24 March 2019.

51   "Annual Public Debt Management Report 2005." Debt Management Department, Kenya National Treasury, 1 June 2005. Retrieved 24 March 2019.

52   "Annual Public Debt Management Report 2011." Debt Management Department, Kenya National Treasury, 1 June 2012. Retrieved 24 March 2019.

53   "Kenya Public Debt." Central Bank of Kenya, 1 September 2018. Retrieved 24 March 2019.

54   "China Top Creditor for Kenya." *Business Daily Africa*, 28 February 2019. Retrieved 24 March 2019.

55   Kenyatta, Uhuru Muigai. 10 June 2010. "Budget Speech for the Fiscal Year 2010/2011." PDF. Wayback Machine. Archived from the original PDF on 30 August 2011.

56   https://web.archive.org/web/20120405063226/http://www.economicstimulus.go.ke/index. php?option=com_content&view=article&id=102&Itemid=226. Archived from the original on 5 April 2012. Retrieved 10 September 2015.

57 "Republic of Kenya: Ministry of Finance." Finance.go.ke. Retrieved 2 August 2011.

58 Nicholas Kerandi. "IFMIS re-engineered to revitalize public financial management." Pfmr. go.ke. Archived from the original on 25 March 2012. Retrieved 2 August 2011.

59 "Capital Business." Capitalfm.co.ke. Archived from the original on 5 May 2011. Retrieved 2 August 2011.

60 http://www.brookings.edu/~/media/research/files/papers/2009/1/kenya-aid-mwega/01_ kenya_aid_mwega.pdf.

61 Mariarosaria. "Kenya Economy." www.italafricacentrale.com. Retrieved 29 October 2018.

62 https://www.cia.gov/library/publications/the-world-factbook/geos/ug.html. Uganda country profile, CIA World Factbook.

63 https://www.cia.gov/library/publications/the-world-factbook/geos/rw.html. Rwanda country profile, CIA World Factbook.

64 Mukherjee, Aparajita, and Saumya Chakrabarti. 16 May 2016. "Development Economics: A Critical Perspective." In Arabic. PHI Learning Pvt. Ltd. ISBN 978-81-203-5219-3.

65 "Archived copy." Archived from the original on 6 November 2018. Retrieved 11 December 2018.

66 "Labor force participation rate, female (% of female population ages 15+) (modeled ILO estimate)." Retrieved 11 June 2015.

67 "Kenya Economic Update: Kenya at work: Energizing the economy and creating jobs." World Bank. December 2012.

68 Ronald Hope Sr, Kempe. "Informal economic activity in Kenya: benefits and drawbacks." African Geographical Review 33/1 (2014): 67–80.

69 Barasa, Fred Simiyu, and Eleanor SM Kaabwe. "Fallacies in policy and strategies of skills training for the informal sector: evidence from the jua kali sector in Kenya." *Journal of Education and Work* 14/3 (2001): 329–53.

70 Ellis, Amanda. *Gender and economic growth in Kenya: Unleashing the power of women.* World Bank Publications, 2007.

71 Sunday, Frankline. "Insecurity holding back Kenya' growth." *The Standard.* Retrieved 20 February 2020.

OTHER REFERENCES

"Life Lessons of an Immigrant." John Makilya, December 2017. https://www. archwaypublishing.com/Bookstore/BookDetail.aspx?Book=762260.

"How Bees Make Honey." https://honeybee.org.au/education/wonderful-world-of-honey/how-bees-make-honey/.

"Type of Bees." https://honeybee.org.au/education/wonderful-world-of-honey/the-type-of-bees/.

"Markets and Chair, Global Accounts Committee." 2018.

"Forbes Technology Council." 2019.

"Despite Good Intentions—Why Development Assistance To The Third World Has Failed." Thomas W. Dichter. 1999.